APOCALYPSE NOW?

£ 3

How may people of faith respond wisely, constructively, and courageously to the challenges of a time of terror? How might religious reasons in public debate be a force for reconciliation rather than violence and hatred?

In a world in which religious arguments and religious motivations play such a huge public role, there is an urgent responsibility for interpreting what is happening, and engaging with religious views which are commonly regarded as alien, threatening or dangerous.

In *Apocalypse Now?*, Duncan Forrester argues that disorders and atrocities which include the Gulag, the Holocaust, 9/11, the Afghanistan and Iraq wars, and the Tsunami disaster have shown us that we stand not at the end of history but in the midst of an apocalyptic age of terror which has striking similarities to the time in which Christianity was born.

Moving between two times of terror – the early Centuries of Christianity, and today – Forrester asks how religious motivations can play a positive role in the midst of conflicts and disasters. Reading the 'signs of the times' to try to understand what is happening in today's age of terror, Forrester argues that there are huge resources in the Christian tradition that can be productively deployed for a more constructive and faithful response. We are at a turning point – this is a book which should be read.

D0257404

For my little Granddaughters
Hannah, Ailsa, Katie and Mairi
That they may live and flourish
In times of Peace rather than of Terror

Apocalypse Now?

Reflections on Faith in a Time of Terror

DUNCAN B. FORRESTER
New College, University of Edinburgh

ASHGATE

© Duncan B. Forrester 2005

Published by
Ashgate Publishing Limited
Gower House
Croft Road
Aldershot
Hants GU11 3HR
England

Ashgate Publishing Company
Suite 420
101 Cherry Street
Burlington, VT 05401-4405
USA

Ashgate website: http://www.ashgate.com

British Library Cataloguing in Publication Data
Forrester, Duncan B., 1933–
  Apocalypse Now? : reflections on faith in a time of terror
  1. war – Religious aspects – Christianity 2. Disasters – Religious aspects –
  Christianity 3. Terrorism – Religious aspects – Christianity 4. Christianity and
  politics 5. Christian ethics 6. Just war doctrine
  I. Title
  261.8'73

Library of Congress Cataloging-in-Publication Data
Forrester, Duncan B., 1933–
  Apocalypse Now? : reflections on faith in a time of terror / Duncan B. Forrester.
    p. cm.
  Includes bibliographical references (p.   ) and index.
  ISBN 0-7546-5260-2 (hardcover:alk. paper) – ISBN 0-7546-5273-4 (pbk.:alk. paper)
  1. Terrorism–Religious aspects–Christianity. 2. Violence–Religious aspects–
  Christianity. 3. Church and social problems. I. Title.

  BT736.15.F67 2005
  261.8'73–dc22

2005007231

ISBN 0 7546 5260 2 (Hbk)
ISBN 0 7546 5273 4 (Pbk)

Printed and bound in Great Britain by TJ International Ltd, Padstow, Cornwall

Contents

Foreword

This book represents one person's reflections on the awesome and confusing events which have followed the 9/11 attacks on the Twin Towers and the Pentagon, and then on the natural but apocalyptic catastrophe that hit the countries around the Indian Ocean on the day after Christmas Day, in 2004, the day when Christians commemorate Stephen, the first Christian martyr. This book makes no claim to being a systematic theological response to a series of events of incredible savagery and violence, but it has been suggested to me that my reflections, however fragmentary, might be of use and interest to others who are trying to relate faith to these awful events, who are seeking to 'discern the signs of the times', and respond appropriately.

My debts in writing this book are many. Some parts of it in an early form were the substance of the Ferguson Lectures which I delivered in the University of Manchester in 2003. I am deeply grateful to Professor Elaine Graham and her colleagues, and those who attended the lectures, for their hospitality and for many helpful discussions. Other parts in an early form were given as the Boutwood Lectures at Corpus Christi College, Cambridge in the spring of 2004. The College welcomed me as a Visiting Fellow for a term, and I had many stimulating discussions with members of the College, particularly with the post-graduate students who lived with me on the Leckhampton campus. This term gave me a precious opportunity for reading and writing, and I am grateful to the Master, Professor Haroun Ahmed, and his colleagues for their hospitality. I also enjoyed discussing the contents of this book with staff and students at Liverpool Hope University, where I was a Visiting Professor in Session 2003–4.

I am grateful to the many colleagues, students and friends who have challenged, confirmed, or enriched my thinking, particularly research students from contemporary apocalyptic situations such as the Rwanda genocide, post-tsunami Sri Lanka, apartheid South Africa, the oppression of Dalits in India, or inter-religious conflict in northern Nigeria. Colleagues and friends such as Dr Michael Northcott, Dr Paul Middleton, Professor Will Storrar, Professor Chris Rowland and Dr Cecilia Clegg have been generous with their time. But above all, the wisdom and discernment of my wife, Margaret, underlies all I do, and in this case her hand can be particularly clearly seen in the postscript on the tsunami. I am grateful to all these, and many others, who are attempting to discern the signs of the times in this age of terror, and how to respond with faith.

Duncan B. Forrester

Acknowledgments

I am grateful to the following for permission to use copyright material:

Faber and Faber Ltd for the extract from T.S. Eliot's *Murder in the Cathedral* in chapter seven; A.P. Watt Ltd for the extracts from W.B. Yeats' poem 'The Second Coming' in chapters one and two; Revd Dr John Bell for his meditation on the tsunami which was originally broadcast on BBC TV; Sage Publications for material in chapters seven and eight derived from my article, 'Violence and Non-violence in Conflict Resolution: Some Theological Reflections', originally published in *Studies in Christian Ethics*, vol. 16 no. 2, pp. 64–79 1963, and Godfrey Rust for his poem which appears at the end of chapter five.

Prologue: Two 'Terrible Manifestos'?

1914

On the day in 1914 when the First World War broke out, a group of 93 leading German intellectuals issued a statement giving unqualified support to the war policy of Kaiser Wilhelm II. The young pastor of Safenwil in Switzerland, Karl Barth by name, who had recently completed his theological studies in Germany, read this 'terrible manifesto', and discovered to his dismay among the signatories almost all his German theological teachers. 'It was,' he wrote, 'like the twilight of the gods when I saw the reaction of Harnack, Herrmann, Rade, Eucken and company to the new situation.'[1] Theological scholarship, it seemed to Barth, had been converted into an ideological weapon of war, and his teachers had been fundamentally compromised. This ethical and political failure, he believed, called into question the theology he had been taught, and 'a whole world of exegesis, ethics, dogmatics and preaching, which I had hitherto held to be essentially trustworthy, was shaken to the foundations, and with it all the other writings of the German theologians'.[2] Schleiermacher, the father of German liberal theology, was, Barth believed, 'unmasked'. A new and very different theological beginning must now be made.

Barth's distress was not because he was a pacifist, opposed to violence and coercion on principle in all situations. He never was a pacifist in the thoroughgoing or principled sense, but he continued to wrestle with the theology and ethics of particular wars and acts of violence throughout his life. Indeed, in the early days of the Second World War, Barth himself issued rousing theologically grounded calls to Christians in France and Britain and the United States to take up arms against Nazism. It was rather that, in 1914, the young Barth saw the liberal theology that almost all his teachers in Germany shared had come to do little more than reflect and reinforce the assumptions and purposes of the German state, giving an aura of holiness to its bellicose military and political purposes. Theology, he believed, had, as it were, been enlisted into the army, where it was under

---

1   Letter to W. Spoendlin, 4 January, 1915, quoted in E. Busch (1976), *Karl Barth: His Life from Letters and Autobiographical Texts*, London: SCM Press, p.81.
2   *Nachwort*, 293, cited in Busch (1976), p.81.

1

orders to act as the ideological wing of the state. Its prophetic voice was silenced, and its arguments had scant reference to the gospel of the Prince of Peace. Instead theology issued a singularly unqualified call to arms. Barth responded by affirming that only a theology which returned to basics, and re-entered 'the strange new world of the Bible' would be capable of making a proper response to the conflicts and hostilities of the day. A new or renewed theology that was far more critical, and suspicious of the intentions of politicians, and sensitive to the ambiguities of politics was required; indeed what was needed, Barth believed, was a theology which actually proclaimed the gospel in the circumstances of the day, and denounced sin, aggressive violence, and the arrogance and idolatry of power.

A very similar situation was to be found in Britain at the time, with prominent churchmen and theologians declaring the war against Germany to be a holy war. The Bishop of London called on every able-bodied man to fight for God and country, and wrote to the *Guardian* in 1915, proclaiming that it was the Church's duty 'to mobilise the nation for a holy war'. In a now notorious Advent sermon he called on British soldiers in the field 'to kill the good as well as the bad, to kill the young men as well as the old'.[3] And in the Second World War no less a figure than William Temple, Archbishop of York and then of Canterbury, and one of the most influential theologians of his day, argued first in traditional just war terms that civilian deaths were permitted provided only that they were not directly made targets, but later on he agreed with Churchill that civilians and non-combatants might be intentionally made targets because in modern total war the distinction between combatants and civilians has been radically eroded.[4]

Theology, Barth realized in 1914, must operate in a different way. It should provide a distinctive and challenging discernment of 'the signs of the times', and call believers to new patterns of costly obedience. It should not collude in the often shady purposes of 'The Powers' or amplify their voice, at that time an unambiguous clarion call to battle. It should rather speak clearly and faithfully with its own voice. Barth's reaction to the pro-war letter of his liberal theological teachers has been argued to be the single most significant turning point of twentieth-century theology.

9/11

In February 2002, in response to the terrorist atrocities of 9/11, a group of some 60 leading American intellectuals, including a number of prominent

---

3   Adrian Hastings (1986), *A History of English Christianity 1920–1985*, London: Jonathan Cape, p.45.

4   Nigel Biggar, 'Anglican Theology of War and Peace', *Crucible*, Oct.–Dec. 2004, p.9.

theologians and church leaders, signed a 'Letter from America: What We Are Fighting For', which was drafted by Professor Jean Bethke Elshtain, the Laura Spelman Rockefeller Professor of Social and Political Ethics in the University of Chicago Divinity School. Professor Elshtain also wrote a book with a significant title, expanding and explaining the position taken up in the Letter, *Just War Against Terror: The Burden of American Power in a Violent World.*[5] After declaring that 'We are united in our belief that invoking God's authority to kill or maim human beings is immoral and is contrary to faith in God',[6] the signatories appeal to the tradition of the just war and say that, 'there are times when waging war is not only morally permitted, but morally necessary, as response to calamitous acts of violence, hatred and injustice. This is one of these times'.[7] Apparently waging a 'just war' in the course of which many innocent non-combatants will be killed is acceptable provided the name of God is not invoked.

The Letter seeks to make clear the reasons for which America has gone to war against 'Terror': 'We fight,' the signatories declare, 'to defend ourselves and to defend ... universal principles'. These universal principles include that all human beings are born free and equal, that government should 'protect and foster the conditions for human flourishing', freedom of conscience and religion, the affirmation that human beings naturally 'seek the truth about life's purpose and ultimate ends', and that 'killing in the name of God is contrary to faith in God and is the greatest betrayal of the universality of religious faith'.[8] The issue, it appears, is not simply self-defence. America is founded 'directly and explicitly on the basis of universal human values', and the struggle is therefore to protect these key values, which 'do not belong only to America, but are in fact the shared inheritance of humankind, and therefore a possible basis of hope for a world community based on peace and justice'.[9] This is not a crusade, but it is certainly presented as a Manichaean ideological conflict, in which the unambiguously good confronts the totally evil. Thus the signatories conclude, 'with one voice we say solemnly that it is crucial for our nation and its allies to win this war. We fight to defend ourselves, but we also believe that we fight to defend those universal principles of

---

5 Elshtain, Jean Bethke (2003), *Just War Against Terror: The Burden of American Power in a Violent World*, New York: Basic Books. Signatories of the Letter included, in addition to Elshtain, Amitai Etzioni, Francis Fukuyama, Os Guiness, Mary Ann Glendon, Samuel Huntington, James Turner Johnson, Richard J. Mouw, Michael Novak, Robert Putnam, Max Stackhouse, Michael Walzer, George Weigel and John Witte, Jnr.
6 Elshtain, p.186.
7 Elshtain, p.189.
8 Elshtain, pp.182–3.
9 Elshtain, p.185.

human rights and human dignity that are the best hope for humankind'.[10]

The Letter appears to offer unconditional support to the American-led 'war on terror'. It operates with a somewhat simplistic view of democracy and its excellences and has little of the suspicion of power and the need for humility on the part of the powerful that we can find in the Christian realism of Reinhold Niebuhr and his school of Christian Realism. There is hardly any theology to be found, at least on the surface of the Letter, and as a consequence it manages to say little that is in any way distinctively Christian, or to call on the profound insights of the gospel. As a consequence it throws little light on why 9/11 happened, or how it is to be understood, except as an unqualified and unintelligible evil.

The *burden* of American power of which the letter speaks is like 'the white man's burden' of the old British Empire, suggesting that the imperial power is acting, not for its own economic and political interests, but on behalf of the subjected people, and indeed of all humankind. The 'burden' is to bring order, justice, security and peace to the world, however much it may cost. And the ultimate goal is assumed to be to educate subject peoples so that they may in course of time possess freedom, democracy and independence – all modelled on the American type of liberal democracy, which is assumed to be without fundamental defects or ambiguities. This is a classic approach of imperial powers seeking to justify their dominance over others, much used by Britain in the heyday of its empire.

Furthermore it is assumed throughout the 'Letter from America, What We're Fighting For', that *war* is the appropriate response to terror. As a citizen of a country which has had its own share of terror, I shudder to think what would have been the outcome if Britain had declared 'war' on the IRA, bombarded its strongholds in Belfast and South Antrim, and invaded Dublin. Britain came fairly close to this under Margaret Thatcher, who tried to stop anyone from talking to the IRA, and declared them all to be 'terrorists'. The short step from this to waging war on terror was taken in events such as 'Bloody Sunday', which not only resulted in numerous civilian casualties, but made progress towards a resolution of the underlying issues far more difficult. The possibility that terrorism should be treated as criminal and dealt with through legal processes while seeking political, economic and social ways forward in relation to the underlying issues is strangely not even mentioned in the Elshtain letter.

In the view of Sir Michael Howard, the doyen of British historians of war, the 'war' on terror has been 'a terrible and irrevocable error' from the start. The British in their time had fought many 'wars' against terrorists, in Palestine, Ireland, Cyprus and Malaysia, but they labelled them 'emergencies', never 'wars'. 'This meant that the police and intelligence services were

---

10   Elshtain, p.193.

provided with exceptional powers, and were reinforced where necessary by the armed forces, but all continued to operate within a peacetime framework of civil authority.' The rhetoric of war tends to create a 'war psychosis' that is wholly counterproductive for the strategic objective of winning 'hearts and minds' in order to deprive the militant networks of local support. Above all, talk of war raised unrealistic and inappropriate expectations, according to Howard: 'The qualities needed in a serious campaign against terrorists – secrecy, intelligence, political sagacity, quiet ruthlessness, covert actions that remain covert, above all infinite patience – all these are forgotten or overridden in a media-stoked frenzy for immediate results, and nagging complaints if they do not get them.'[11]

The American Letter appears to give as unqualified endorsement to the 'War against Terror' as the letter signed by the leading German intellectuals had done some 90 years before in relation to the First World War.[12] In November 2002, a group of nine of the original signatories of the Letter from America, including two theologians, issued a statement on 'Pre-emption, Iraq and Just War: A Statement of Principle', in which they gave qualified support to an attack on Iraq if it did not cooperate in arms inspections or comply with UN resolutions. They appeared also to support in certain circumstances pre-emptive strikes and a kind of regime change, although within a central restraint of traditional just war thinking, the insistence on 'last resort': 'As President Bush recently stated, true disarmament in Iraq would constitute "regime change" in its most relevant aspect – it would dramatically reduce Saddam Hussein's capacity to threaten his neighbours and the world. That should be the principal aim of U.S. policy, and we should resort to war only if we have exhausted all other reasonable means of achieving it.'[13]

Interestingly enough, both American letters are singularly short of theology. Indeed the nearest Elshtain comes to explicit theology in her Letter is the defence of separation of church and state in America, which is seen as one of the precious gifts that America is now generously sharing with the rest of the world.

As had been the case with the German intellectuals' letter of 1914, the American Letter of 2002 found its critics, most notably Stanley Hauerwas

---

11 See Professor Sir Michael Howard's incisive article, 'Mistake to Declare this a War', *Royal United Services Institute Journal*, Dec. 2001.

12 Note that this time the Letter from America elicit a vigorous response signed by more than one hundred German intellectuals: *A World of Justice and Peace Would be Different*, available at http://www.americanvalues.org/html/german_statement.html, and the response by the Americans, 'Is the Use of Force Ever Morally Justified?' which seeks to confine the discussion to the issue of pacifism: http://www.americanvalues.org/html/is_the_use_of_force_ever_moral.html.

13 'Pre-emption, Iraq and Just War', 14 Nov. 2002.

and Paul Griffiths, who produced a peculiarly sharp response to Elshtain's book which expounded the Letter.[14] Hauerwas and Griffiths accuse her not only of affirming the right of self-defence, but of endorsing pre-emptive strikes and the strategy of 'regime change'. This amounts, they say, to a 'new imperialism' which 'means that the more a state diverges from American principles, the more pressing will be America's duty to remake it in its own image'. Elshtain is accused of a taking up a position which is virtually identical to the National Security Strategy of the Bush Administration. America should intervene militarily when she judges a state to have 'failed': the kind of imperialistic intervention advocated by Michael Ignatieff and others. 'Her work,' they say, 'is ideology masquerading as dispassionate analysis'.[15] She does not consider the possibility that a 'war on terror' is not the most appropriate response to a huge crime like 9/11: 'You do not go to war against murderers', Hauerwas and Griffith, in agreement with Michael Howard, declare, 'Instead you try to arrest them.'[16]

Above all, Hauerwas and Griffiths echo in a new context Barth's 1914 accusation that his theological teachers had abandoned serious and critical Christian theology in order to give unqualified support to military and chauvinist ideologies and courses of action. They accuse Elshtain and her co-signatories of recognizing little or no distinction between the way Christians and Americans should think about the 'war on terror', and finally they declare that the use of Christian language and ideas in Elshtain's book is nothing more than window dressing for 'a passion to impose America upon the world'.[17]

Without necessarily endorsing in detail Barth's critique of his liberal theological teachers in 1914, or the attack of Stanley Hauerwas and Paul Griffiths on Jean Elshtain's book and the Letter signed by leading American intellectuals, I agree with them that, in times of conflict, violence and terror such as the present there is an urgent need for serious *theological* engagement with the issues, attempting to discern the signs of the times and suggest the most appropriate responses for disciples – and also for 'The Powers'. At the start of such a process, we have to set aside Manichaean assumptions that our democratic societies are good and innocent, and those who criticize and those who attack them are obviously and totally evil and wrong. Before we make theological and political judgments about how most appropriately to respond to awful and portentous events such as 9/11, we need to attempt to understand, for instance, why young Palestinians were dancing

---

14 In *First Things*, Oct. 2003, no. 136, pp.41–4. Elshtain's incandescent response is on pp.44–6.
15 *First Things*, p.42.
16 *First Things*, p.43.
17 *First Things*, pp.43–4.

and singing in the streets for joy when they heard news of the attacks on the twin towers and the Pentagon. Very uncomfortable facts have to be faced, and the ambiguities of the political sphere have to be acknowledged, as they were in an earlier generation by Reinhold Niebuhr and others. Above all, the 'battle for hearts and minds' has to be 'fought' and won. And this is only possible if we start by asking very seriously why there is such antagonism and hatred directed towards the West, and America in particular.

The Manichaean streak in American politics – we are innocent and our antagonists are wholly evil – was understandably reinforced by the struggle against Nazism, and by the horrors of the Holocaust. The demand for unconditional surrender was a reflection of this Manichaean attitude: absolute evil must not be compromised with. It was further strengthened by the Cold War, with Communism presented as the Great Satan. The collapse of 1989 was widely understood in America as another unqualified and total victory over evil. But such an unqualified victory over 'terror' is impossible, even if the main assaults are on states or regimes which are believed to harbour terrorist networks.

What I miss from the theologians who signed the Letter is serious and distinctive critical theology after the style of Reinhold Niebuhr and others. Niebuhr was as committed to democracy as Elshtain and her colleagues. His little 1945 'vindication' of democracy, *The Children of Light and the Children of Darkness*,[18] famously declares that 'Man's capacity for justice makes democracy possible; but man's inclination to injustice makes democracy necessary.'[19] Yet Niebuhr is constantly aware of the ambiguities of democratic systems and his vindication of democracy is worlds apart from the panegyric of the American style of liberal democracy that we find in the intellectuals' Letter. Niebuhr also constantly emphasizes that the possession of power aggravates the sinful human tendency to deal unjustly and proudly with others. 'That,' he writes, 'is why irresponsible and uncontrolled power is the greatest source of injustice.' Theologians should, in this context, be asking hard questions about the only surviving superpower and its purposes and practices from long before 9/11.

Elshtain's account of Tillich and Niebuhr's attitude to the Nazi regime before and during the Second World War is illuminating. They took sides unambiguously against the horrors of Nazism, while remaining suspicious of every manifestation of a Manichaean division of the world into the absolutely good and the absolutely evil. Niebuhr in particular was towards the end of the war peculiarly sensitive to the dangers of the power of the victors corrupting their behaviour and making them oppressive.

---

18 Reinhold Niebuhr (1945), *The Children of Light and the Children of Darkness*, London: Nisbet.

19 Ibid., p.vi.

Good News?

This book is an attempt by one Christian theologian to begin the complex
and confusing task of reading 'the signs of the times'. This I do by moving
between two times of terror – the early centuries of Christianity, and today
– in the hope that this may give some clues as to how to understand what
is happening and how most appropriately, constructively and faithfully to
respond. First, I explore in general terms the two times of terror, seeking
for similarities and differences. The good news of Jesus Christ emerged in
a time of terror. The light shone in the darkness, and the darkness did not
overcome it (John 1.5). Does that light continue to shine in the darkness of
today and, if so, how?

There is certainly plenty of bad news around these days. Some of us
hesitate to turn on the radio news, or open the paper, because there seems
to be a kind of limit to the bad news we can absorb and deal with. Some
of us are old enough to remember the appalling film footage of the freshly
liberated extermination camps shown in the cinemas immediately after the
Second World War, 'lest we forget'. We are still coming to terms with the
Holocaust and wrestling with the terrible question of how one can speak of
God, and of good news, after Auschwitz. And then the awful truth of the
Gulag in the old Soviet Union unfolded before our eyes as we listened to
Pasternak and Solzhenitsyn telling us of their experiences, and of the
millions of others who were humiliated, degraded, starved and worked to
death in the camps in what had been regarded by many as a beacon of
hope, anticipating the future for humankind, 'a new civilization' as Sidney
and Beatrice Webb called it.

The end of the Cold War and the collapse of the communist dictatorships
seemed at first to be unqualified good news, but it was quickly overtaken
by the outbreaks of internecine violence in the Balkans, the massacre of
7300 Muslim men and boys at Srebrenica in 1995. In Palestine and Israel
vengeance and retribution spiral constantly out of control, with rage and
despair turning perfectly normal children into suicide bombers, while
sophisticated armaments supplied by the United States are used to devastate
and attack refugee camps and kill innocent men, women and children as
well as militants. The war in Afghanistan was bad enough. Then we had
the daily horrors of the Iraq War and the continuing bloody occupation of
that country. Terrorist outrages, so fearfully predictable, mean that millions
walk in fear while their leaders seem incapable of an understanding, prudent
and just response. Rage, despair, hatred and immense cruelty characterize
the end of an era in which many people, in the West at least, expected the
new Jerusalem to be builded here. The very values that the 'war on terror'
is said to defend are sacrificed in Guantanamo Bay and Abu Ghraib prison,
and many another place. There does not appear to be much good news

around. We all – Christian believers, and others as well – have immense difficulty in making sense of it all, in finding God in the imbroglio of today's awesome events, in daring to speak of the gospel, or to believe that there is in fact 'good news'.

Those who believed in a worldwide rapid and remorseless decline of religion in face of modernity, enlightenment, rationality and the scientific spirit have had in recent times to recognize, often with a mixture of puzzlement and dismay, that religion in a huge variety of diverse forms not only survives but grows and flourishes. People today can sensibly speak of the 'desecularization of the world'.[20] Globally religion does not survive timidly in the private and domestic sphere; it is rampant today in the public sphere all over the world. And those who saw religion as fairly uniformly sweetness and light, a benign and peaceable force for good – perhaps the basis for 'global ethics', as Hans Küng argues – have had to face the fact that there is in many situations today, as always, a strong alliance between religion and violence, religion and terror, religion and rage.[21] To believers, their religion represents truth and is a powerful determinant of behaviour, but religion and religious arguments can also, of course, be used to enrage, to disguise what is really happening, and to encourage people in radically evil courses.

Christians believe in the gospel; that is, that they have good news to proclaim and offer, even – perhaps especially – in times of despair and fear. The Christian gospel initially appeared in a time of terror, with striking similarities to today. Can we recover the ability to discern and proclaim good news in a world that is full of violence and despair and evil, when all the news appears to be bad? In handling this question we need to look backwards to the early years of the faith to see if we can learn lessons that are relevant to today's context from the way the faith was presented and shaped two thousand years ago. And then we need to look seriously at today's situation with its challenges and opportunities for the proclamation of good news.

Christian Public Theology for long engaged in a dialogue with the great ideologies, particularly Marxism, democratic liberalism and neoconservatism. These debates continue to be important, but it is a central argument of this book that Public Theology must engage today far more directly and urgently with the realities of religion in all their diversity and power, and with theologies some of which may seem primitive and savage, but which have a continuing power to touch the heart and elicit courage, brutality and self-sacrifice as well as love and a passion for justice.

---

20 See the essays in Peter Berger (ed.) (1999), *The Desecularization of the World: Resurgent Religion and World Politics*, Grand Rapids: Eerdmans.

21 See René Girard (1977), *Violence and the Sacred*, Baltimore: Johns Hopkins University Press.

I think there is a threefold responsibility laid upon the shoulders of religious people and theologians, particularly in the West, today:

a To interpret to our secular societies the continuing power, significance and meaning of religious discourse about, and in, the public sphere. This must not neglect religious discourse of an apparently extreme form, but should try to explain why it has such influence for many in today's world.

b To engage in direct, and sometimes hard-hitting, dialogue within and between religions. This is not simply a matter of identifying some generally agreed ethical commonalities of a broad sort, as in Hans Küng's project of a 'Global Ethics'. Fundamental differences have to be faced and discussed, as well as the evil effects of some of these views and positions.

c To avoid the idealism which does not take interest, sin and brokenness seriously in the efforts to produce good out of the political process in the world's rather wild political arena. Eschatology, hope, aspirations and goals are of the greatest importance. But Public Theology must also have a dimension of realism if it is to operate effectively for good in a world which still 'waits with eager longing for the revealing of the children of God' (Romans 8.19).

Chapter 1

Vexed by a Rocking Cradle

> The darkness drops again but now I know
> That twenty centuries of stony sleep
> Were vexed to nightmare by a rocking cradle.[1]

The Christian gospel came first in an age of terror, when multitudes and, particularly, the authorities were vexed to nightmare by the world in which they lived and by a particular rocking cradle. Jesus, according to Luke's gospel, was born in Bethlehem rather than his home town of Nazareth, because of an autocratic imperial decree from a despotic foreign government. Again according to the tradition, shortly after his birth he was visited and honoured by Magi, or 'kings', from the East who recognized on behalf of the Gentile world his cosmic and earthly status as Messiah and Prince of Peace. The enquiries of the Magi in Jerusalem provoked desperate and draconian measures on the part of the Roman stooge, King Herod, who initiated in Bethlehem the 'massacre of the innocents', at the time just one of many massacres of innocent people on the part of political and religious authorities. The baby in Bethlehem was seen from the beginning, the tradition suggests, as a threat to established authority and the existing order, political and religious.

The massacre of the innocents in Bethlehem on the order of Herod was just a typical example of what today would be called state-sponsored terror. Herod was both a ruthless tyrant and a collaborator with the alien Roman regime. The child Jesus was, we are told, taken to Egypt as a refugee, an asylum seeker, from Herod's wrath by Mary and Joseph.

The teaching of Jesus and the movement that gathered around him were seen consistently as spiritual and religious threats, which were also political challenges which had to be dealt with. The Roman Empire, in all its provinces, was full of torture, injustice and exploitation. The Pax Romana was substantially built on terror and intimidation. The ultimate, horrifying penalty of crucifixion was freely used, especially with dissidents and rebels. Thus the crucifixion of Jesus was no unusual event; thousands of slaves were crucified along the Appian Way in the aftermath of the revolt led by Spartacus, and Jesus was crucified along with two criminals. Unjustly

---

1 W.B. Yeats, 'The Second Coming', 1919. Written shortly before the start of a peculiarly bloody civil war in Ireland.

condemned by the Roman Procurator, Pilate, Jesus was scourged, tortured and executed in the most hideous way imaginable. Mel Gibson's controversial film is realistic in its depiction of crucifixion – too much so for many. We have difficulty in coping with such terror and so much vindictive cruelty, just as we have difficulty in responding wisely and well to the terror and the horrors of the world today. We suffer from compassion fatigue, and our anger seems to achieve nothing.

Jesus: Witness to Truth[2]

John's gospel depicts the trial of Jesus before Pilate as a direct confrontation between the One who has been declared to be the embodiment of truth, and the ultimate political power in the conquered land of Israel. It was also a confrontation between two very different understandings of politics. The Jews take Jesus before Pilate because they do not wish to be responsible for the execution of Jesus, and they are unwilling to be defiled ritually. There then takes place between Pilate and the chief priests a struggle of jurisdictions, otherwise called evading responsibility, or passing of the buck.

Pilate as the judge assumes that he is dealing with a petty, domestic Jewish religious squabble rather than a cosmic event. Power, represented by Pilate, confronts truth, represented by Jesus. 'Are you the King of the Jews? A political threat? Seditious?' asks Pilate. Jesus stands silent, as if to question Pilate's jurisdiction. Pilate presses on with his examination: 'What have you done? What is your offence? How do you plead?' Jesus responds, somewhat obliquely: 'My kingdom is not from this world. It doesn't follow the rules of worldly politics, with fighting, violence, coercion as the ultimate sanction.' 'Ah,' says Pilate, 'so you *are* a king then; you are a politician; you are a threat to the established order.' 'Your word,' says Jesus (note that he does not deny being a king, or being relevant to the political order), 'I came into the world to testify, to witness (*martureso*) to the Truth. Everyone who belongs to the Truth hears my voice.'

Pilate asks the rhetorical question so beloved of academics, an abstract, free-floating question detached from the personal, the concrete, the particular: 'What is Truth?' And then, without pausing for an answer, he proceeds as a politician, as a judge, to fulfil the duty of his office – to determine and declare the truth: 'This man is innocent!' Then Pilate concocts a subtle political compromise; he will release Jesus who claims to be the Truth, with a vague implication of guilt now lurking about him. And so Pilate hopes to satisfy the people without putting to death a man he

---

2   John 18.28–19.16. I am indebted in this section especially to Lesslie Newbigin (1982), *The Light Has Come*, Grand Rapids: Eerdmans, pp.237–60.

knows to be innocent. But they cry for Barrabas instead. Because he is not of the Truth, Pilate cannot face the hatred of the world which the Truth arouses.[3] He is trapped in his own stratagem, for when the people cry out for Barabbas it is no longer possible for him to set Jesus free. Having failed to acknowledge the Truth, he is in the power of the lie.

Pilate tries another tack. If Jesus, the innocent one, is humiliated, flogged and tortured, perhaps the people will let him release Jesus. But no, the democratic voice is, 'Crucify him.' Pilate tries to shift the buck: 'You take him and crucify him,' he says. Then Pilate is afraid, for he is told that Jesus, like the emperor, claims to be *the* Son of God. Pilate did not need to be reminded that, if he released one who threatened the emperor's throne, he would be 'no friend of Caesar'.

Jesus declares that Pilate's power comes from God, and should be used for God's purposes of good and truth. Pilate presents Jesus to the people: 'Here is your king!' he says. But the chief priests reply, 'We have no king but Caesar.'

There are two understandings of power and politics at work in this narrative. Pilate is deflected into denying the Truth by a common language of politics which prioritizes expediency and personal advantage over Truth. Pilate betrays his trust and betrays the Truth. In order to do this one has to assume that the question, 'What is Truth?' is unanswerable or that 'the sword of truth' can be manipulated for sordid purposes. The lesson is that truth and truthfulness are necessary in politics, and it makes no sense to ask if what is meant here is *religious* truth, in the narrow modern sense; it is truth *simpliciter*. The paradoxical truth is that politics is not about the reversal of the power structures of today, but about the transfiguration of politics by the rule of the Lamb that has been slain, and is now, despite appearances, on the throne.[4]

And vocation, calling, as of Pilate as judge, is necessary in any decent society, and carries with it its own imperatives. But we are not speaking here of some free-standing common morality, but rather of something that needs constant challenge, refreshment and limitation from the Truth. A sense of calling carries with it a sense of accountability to more than the popular will. For one in authority is responsible to more than a democratic majority, but indeed to the Truth.

And then there came the Resurrection and the development and spread throughout the Empire of the Church, which continued to vex, in its own distinctive way, the established order of things in religion and social and political life alike.

---

3 John 7.7.

4 On this theme see especially John Howard Yoder (1988), 'To Serve our God and to Rule the World', *The Annual of the Society of Christian Ethics*, pp.3–14.

Empire and Collaborators

The Roman Empire, which spread around the Mediterranean basin and beyond, built on the conquests of Alexander the Great and his successors, the Ptolemaic and Seleucid rulers of the fragments of the Empire Alexander had established by force of arms. The Romans gradually, especially after the conquest of Carthage, built up a colossal empire and by 63BC they controlled the whole of the Eastern Mediterranean. They established the so-called 'Pax Romana', which was based very largely upon terror, although it also allowed the development of trade and commerce around the Mediterranean and the Black Sea, and far beyond.

This was also a time of economic exploitation, by the Romans and their allies, as resources were drained from the periphery of the Empire to Rome itself. And even the temple in Jerusalem which Jesus 'purged' had become a symbol and exemplar of economic exploitation of the people. Jesus' action in the Temple was a challenge to an interlocking system of political, economic and religious control.

Many parts of the Empire, like the various territories which made up Palestine, were mainly ruled by local collaborators, a political arrangement that in the heyday of the British Empire was called 'indirect rule'. Jewish society was thus controlled largely by the collaborating Herodian kings, a self-serving Jewish aristocracy, and a deeply compromised priesthood.[5] Sometimes the two forms of regime operated side by side. Consider, for instance, the trial of Jesus before the Jewish Sanhedrin, before the Roman Procurator, Pilate, and before the Jewish collaborator, King Herod. Indirect rule was, and is, an economical and effective way of exercising imperial authority. Sometimes the local rulers who were coopted into this kind of system were deeply hated by their subjects; but often indirect rule gave a plausible suggestion of at least a semblance of independence. And commonly the Romans left much of the really unpleasant work of suppressing the people and putting down uprisings and protests to these local and indigenous rulers.

Thus Herod Antipas, the tetrarch at the time of the birth of Jesus, was a repressive tyrant, whose rule was hated by his own Jewish people, who saw it as a lightly disguised form of foreign Gentile domination and oppression. Herod had an army of non-Jewish mercenaries, a spy system and a secret police.[6] According to the Jewish historian, Josephus, he felt deeply threatened by the multitudes that thronged around John the Baptist, and the gospels tell how he did John to death.

---

5   Richard A. Horsley (1987), *Jesus and the Spiral of Violence: Popular Jewish Resistance in Roman Palestine*, San Francisco: Harper and Row, pp.44–5.
6   Richard A. Horsley (1987), *Jesus and the Spiral of Violence: Popular Jewish Resistance in Roman Palestine*, San Francisco: Harper and Row, pp.44–5.

Terror

Indirect rule was an effective way of cowing an oppressed people with the fear or the reality of terror, sponsored and carried through by the authorities. 'Roman warlords,' writes Horsley, 'used crucifixion as an instrument to terrorise subject peoples into submission to imperial rule.' Roman military terror established the context for the emergence of the Jesus movement. The Roman-sponsored state terror against rebellious Judean and Galilean people 'included thousands enslaved at Magdala/Tarichaea in Galilee in 52–51 BCE, mass enslavement in and around Sepphoris (near Nazareth) and thousands crucified at Emmaus in Judea in 4 BCE, and the systematic devastation of villages and towns, destruction of Jerusalem and the Temple, and mass enslavement in 67–70 CE'.[7]

There were, of course, also resistance movements which often also had recourse to appalling violence – the Zealots, or Sicarii, of Jesus' time come to mind. They specialized in assassinations, especially of members of the high priestly families who collaborated with Rome, and kidnapping in order to obtain the release of captured members of their own group.[8] Their last stand was at Masada, near the Dead Sea. They committed collective suicide with their families before the rocky stronghold fell to the Roman armies in 73 AD. The Zealots drew much of their inspiration from the Maccabean revolt some centuries before, which is recounted in the apocryphal books of the Macabbees. This was against the Ptolemaic and Seleucid heirs of Alexander the Great's empire. Antiochus Epiphanes and others instituted a programme of enforced Hellenization which led to a huge, violent and prolonged culture war led initially, on the Jewish side, by Judas Maccabaeus and his brothers.

Culture Clash

The Christian good news emerged at a time of the clash of cultures, civilizations and religions. Throughout most of the Roman Empire both cultural Hellenism and the official cult of the divine emperor were imposed ruthlessly on subject peoples with all sorts of threats and inducements.

The Maccabean revolts were the most famous and effective ways in which pious Jews violently opposed both Hellenization and the power of the empire. Maccabean saints embraced death as martyrs rather than obey

---

7   Richard A. Horsley (1997) (ed.), *Paul and Empire: Religion and Power in Roman Imperial Society*, Harrisburg: Trinity Press, pp.10–11.

8   Richard A. Horsley (1987), *Jesus and the Spiral of Violence: Popular Jewish Resistance in Roman Palestine*, San Francisco: Harper and Row, pp.40–42.

the imperial order to renounce their faith and its practices. They also fought, ruthlessly and often successfully, against the forces of empire. But to many 'educated' and 'civilized' people at the time it seemed to be a conflict between rationality and fanaticism. The Maccabeans saw themselves as resisting in the name of the God of Israel a ruthless tyranny which was determined to destroy their religion and their culture and make them Hellenes. And there were among the Jews many 'renegades' who welcomed the adoption of Gentile ways and the abandonment of the customs which God had commanded their forebears to keep for ever. 'They built a gymnasium in Jerusalem according to Gentile custom, and removed the marks of circumcision, and abandoned the holy covenant. They joined with the Gentiles and sold themselves to do evil.'[9] The Temple in Jerusalem was profaned and 'on the fifteenth day of Chislev in the one hundred and forty-fifth year [167BC], they erected a desolating sacrilege on the altar of burnt-offering … The books of the law that they found they tore to pieces and burnt with fire … they put to death the women who had their children circumcised, and their families and those who circumcised them; and they hung their infants from their mothers' necks.'[10] But 'many in Israel stood firm and were resolved in their hearts not to eat unclean food. They chose to die rather than to be defiled by food or to profane the holy covenant, and they did die. Very great wrath came upon Israel'.[11]

In response to what they understood as Gentile cultural, religious and political aggression, the Maccabees 'organized an army and struck down sinners in their anger and renegades in their wrath; the survivors fled to the Gentiles for safety. And Mattathias and his friends went around and tore down the altars; they forcibly circumcised all the uncircumcised boys that they found within the borders of Israel. They hunted down the arrogant and the work prospered in their hands'.[12]

Terror and cultural and religious aggression, directly or indirectly on the part of the Empire, were thus met with a violent traditionalist backlash, although 'all the renegade and godless men of Israel' collaborated with the imperial authorities. The Jews, who felt that their faith and their culture were being threatened by the imperial power, hit back with savage violence, and in doing so they were remarkably successful. Many Jews triumphed in dying as martyrs, condemned to an agonizing death by cruel alien tyrants for their adherence to the Law and for their rejection of Hellenizing forces in religion and culture. One of the most detailed and terrible stories of the torture and killing of seven brothers and their mother in II Maccabees 7

---

9   I Maccabees 1. 14–15.
10 I Maccabees 1.54, 56, 59–61.
11 I Maccabees 1.62–4.
12 I Maccabees 2.44–8.

clearly assumes the hope of resurrection for those who are faithful to the Law.

How similar it all sounds to the world today!

Political Religion

There was, of course, a persistent and unavoidable conflict between the developing political religion of the Roman Empire and Jewish faith. In the Empire, piety and patriotism were virtually indistinguishable. In Judaism, on the other hand, the kingship of Yahweh was resolutely affirmed, and all other claims to final authority were firmly denied. Political religion in its simplest form was found in most of the city states of antiquity. The city is watched over by its gods, who share in its joys and sorrows. The cult is an affirmation and a celebration of the life of the city. This kind of religion did not seek to change, challenge or question the established order; rather it proclaims that it is god-given and sacrosanct. The pious person, the good person and the good citizen are all one and the same.

With the growth of the Roman Empire came the development of a highly formal imperial cult which served the turn of a civil religion, eliciting and confirming loyalty to the Empire, but making few and infrequent demands, like Shintoism in modern Japan. Hospitality to and tolerance of a wide range of local cults and mystery religions was in no way incompatible with the maintenance of the syncretistic imperial religion, provided that these other religions made no universal or exclusive claims which conflicted with the special position of the official public religion of the Empire, and were willing to serve as voluntary and mainly local embellishments to the official religion or, like Judaism for long periods of the diaspora, were content to confine themselves and their universalistic claims to a social ghetto from which they posed no threat, protected by law as a *religio licita*.

But this form of symbiosis was difficult in the Promised Land when occupied by a pagan Gentile Empire which for much of the time was active in discouraging and opposing Judaism and in propagating aggressively the religion, customs and cultures which were dominant elsewhere in the Empire. Conflict between the Empire and the faith of Israel, and then of the Church, was almost inevitable. The claims of the emperor were incompatible with the claims of Yahweh.

Vexing Good News

In the midst of all this the Word became flesh, Jesus was executed in agony, and was raised again, disciples gathered together to break bread and worship, and showed themselves willing to die as martyrs rather than deny the good news which they proclaimed with astonishing boldness. Hope overcame despair, and non-violence was shown to be a way forward. The baby in the cradle and the young man on the cross vexed and challenged and rocked the security of the emperor and all his panoply of power, confronted the structures of injustice and oppression, and the lies which supported oppression.

And then there came the Church, a new form of egalitarian and non-hierarchical community, which burst into the Gentile world after being nurtured in the womb of Judaism. From the first it believed that it had good news to proclaim, even, or especially, in a time of terror. The world-view in which it clothed the gospel was apocalyptic, and the whole community was initially nourished on apocalyptic literature. But the early Church had a very different view of violence and of the hope of the coming of the new Jerusalem from most who dwelt in an apocalyptic world.[13] Christians believed that in the life, death and resurrection of Jesus the end time had already come and there was good news to proclaim. It was good news of something that had happened, rather than a new set of laws or ethical injunctions, although to be sure the good news carried with it injunctions to be faithful to the teachings of the Lord. It was good news which nurtured hope in an age when many despaired, and this hope was otherworldly, not in the sense that it regarded what went on in the world as matters of indifference, but rather that God's reign [which] was to be realized in its fullness at the end time. Then a new heaven and earth would be revealed, and the holy city, the home of the faithful, the new Jerusalem would come 'down out of heaven from God, prepared as a bride adorned for her husband'. Then God would make all things new, and wipe away every tear from the eye. The early Christians effectively and dramatically challenged the existing authorities and 'Powers' by calling their claims to ultimacy into question, and showing that there was a better way, which was bound to triumph at the last.

And the early Christians, living in a time of terror, did not only proclaim in words good news of a coming order of peace, justice and love, a new and fresh understanding of community; they exemplified it in their fellowships. According to Tertullian, and many early Christian writers, Christians are 'resident aliens', whose true citizenship is in heaven rather than here:

> We are a body knit together as such by a common religious profession, by unity of discipline, and by the bond of a common hope … Your citizenship, your magistracies, and the very name of your curia is the Church of Christ …

---

13   See especially Revelation 21.

You are an alien in this world, and a citizen of the city of Jerusalem that is above.[14]

'Nothing, Tertullian continued, 'is more foreign to us than the state. One state we know, of which all are citizens'.[15] This did not mean that the early Christians, holding the faith in a time of terror, were detached from the world of politics, from the Empire with its idolatrous claims, from the life of society. In politics, as in private and domestic life, they understood themselves as offering and demonstrating a new and better way, which was neither the path of the violent Zealots, seeking to overthrow the existing order of things, nor passive detachment from the principalities and powers that operate in the public sphere. The rocking cradle and those who found there their truth and hope continued to vex the principalities and powers, and those who live by violence. And yet there was hope, even for the powers whose true mandate was to be servants of God's love and justice.

From the beginning, the Christian Church believed that it had, especially in times of terror, Good News which has a bearing not only on subjectivity and the inner life, but on the public life of the world, on politics and economics in a world that is full of coercion and violence, and fear. The Church has the responsibility to be a faithful steward of the Good News, and to discern the signs of the times with reverence and rigour. Despite appearances, the early Christians believed, God is mysteriously in control, and God's purposes of love, justice and mercy will triumph in the end. In a real sense, their task was to ensure that the world was aware that it was being vexed by a rocking cradle.

In the next chapter I will discuss the conviction, increasingly common in eighteenth-century Europe and America, that religion, especially apocalyptic religion, is the problem, not the solution, and accordingly there was in the Enlightenment project an attempt to establish a rational way of restraining violence and ensuring peace.

---

14   Tertullian (1869–70), *Apologeticus* 39; *De Corona* 13, in *The Writings of Tertullian*, Ante-Nicene Christian Library, 3 vols, Edinburgh: T. & T. Clark.

15   *Apologeticus* 28.

Chapter 2

Things Fall Apart: The Long, Bloody Twentieth Century

> Turning and turning in the widening gyre
> The falcon cannot hear the falconer;
> Things fall apart; the centre cannot hold;
> Mere anarchy is loosed upon the world,
> The blood-dimmed tide is loosed, and everywhere
> The ceremony of innocence is drowned;
> The best lack all conviction, while the worst
> Are full of passionate intensity.[1]

The Enlightenment project, as is well known, was in large part a reaction against the horrors of the 'wars of religion' that had ravaged Europe from the time of the Reformation. This is not to suggest that the crucial figures of the Enlightenment were uniformly opposed to religion in all its forms as the ultimate cause of the distress of Europe. Some, like Voltaire and most of the leading French Enlightenment figures, blamed religion for most of the ills from which Europe suffered, and sought an entirely secular society in Europe. The Scottish Enlightenment as a whole, with the notable exception of David Hume, was far more sympathetic to the Christian faith, and indeed many of its prominent figures were clergymen. But, for all that, they were very critical of the 'fanaticism' and violence that had characterized much Scottish, and European, religion in the seventeenth century.

Immanuel Kant espoused religion and specifically Christianity 'within the limits of reason alone', to quote the title of his famous short treatise. Self-critical religion, for him, had a place in an enlightened society, and his own understanding of religion was Christian, and indeed in some ways specifically Lutheran. Enlightenment, he declares, is not just a response to the terrors of the wars of religion; it 'is man's leaving his self-caused immaturity. Immaturity is the incapacity to use one's intelligence without the guidance of another. Such immaturity is self-caused if it is not caused by lack of intelligence, but by lack of determination and courage to use one's intelligence without being guided by another. *Sapere Aude!* Have the courage

---

1   W.B. Yeats, 'The Second Coming', 1919.

to use your own intelligence is therefore the motto of the enlightenment'.[2]

Humankind, meaning for all practical purposes white middle-class European men, has with the Enlightenment come of age and has passed beyond superstition, or so it was believed. People are now capable of organizing life on a rational basis, unlike the superstition and fanaticism of the days of ignorance, dogma and prejudice of the past. Accordingly, as a kind of crown to his moral and political writings, Kant produces in later life a project for 'Perpetual Peace' between nations (1795). Such perpetual peace should come among enlightened peoples when it takes 'the place of the peacemakings, falsely so-called because really just truces'.[3] Against this kind of rational religion there survived, as a potent source of misunderstanding, obscurantism and conflict, fanatical or 'enthusiastic' religion. But it was generally believed to be in its death throes, having been dealt a fatal blow by enlightenment.

The euphoria of the Enlightenment, as it spread across Europe and North America had many significant accomplishments to its credit, but it did little to question the spread of a rapacious European imperialism in Africa and Asia, or to provide a critique of the horrors of the slave trade, for example. It led to an optimistic and deep-seated conviction that things were getting progressively better – the belief in progress – and that conscientious and thoughtful people could with courage learn to live in peace with one another, and rule beneficently over less enlightened peoples. Above all, there was an air of optimism and a deep belief in progress. The dark days of the past, and in particular of the wars of religion, had been left behind and the world was now a better place in every way. Civilized people are above divisive superstitions and are now able, if they so choose, to live together in peace and harmony.

Things began palpably to 'fall apart' in the early twentieth century. The liberal optimism which became deeply entrenched in the nineteenth century was deeply disturbed by the First World War, a conflict between the most 'advanced' and 'enlightened' powers in the world. This war was fought with unprecedented 'savagery', or 'barbarism', not at all in a 'civilized' or enlightened manner. It was hard for the optimistic nineteenth-century belief that everything was getting better to survive the gory carnage of trench warfare, so vividly portrayed in the novels of Pat Barker's *Regeneration* trilogy. People were deeply disillusioned by the fact that both sides claimed divine sanction for their cause. Young Karl Barth was horrified, as we have seen, by the endorsement by many of his theological teachers of the Kaiser's

---

2   Immanuel Kant, 'What is Enlightenment? [1784]' in Carl J. Friedrich (ed.) (1949), *The Philosophy of Kant: Immanuel Kant's Moral and Political Writings*, New York: Random House, p.132.

3   Immanuel Kant, 'Eternal Peace', in Carl J. Friedrich (ed.), *The Philosophy of Kant: Immanuel Kant's Moral and Political Writings*, New York: Random House, 1949, p.476.

cause. Intellectuals in general, including theologians, seemed incapable of preserving in time of crisis the kind of civilized and critical detachment that was the Enlightenment ideal. Excited theological voices on both sides spoke with 'passionate intensity' in support of their nation's cause. Prophetic and peaceful voices were hardly heard.

It still came as a huge surprise and disappointment that the rise of Hitler and the Nazi movement encountered so little opposition from the 'enlightened' academic world. Indeed many academics, including some prominent theologians, were Nazi supporters or collaborators throughout the Hitler period. The whole Enlightenment project seemed to have disintegrated even in its central bastion. But another, more sinister, explanation for what had happened is possible. Zygmund Bauman in his *Modernity and the Holocaust* (1993) argues that Nazism, and in particular the Holocaust and the camps were an expression of a modernity shaped by the Enlightenment. And in an essay, 'A Century of Camps?' in which he considers the camps as an appalling exemplar of a modernist project, Bauman examines the extermination camps as an extreme case of a perverse desire to have mastery over human nature, human craving and human needs. The camps in this context, he argues, had their own 'sinister rationality'. They were part of an attempt to create a new Europe 'better structured and better organized than before'. And they were intended to fulfil three functions:

> They were laboratories where the new unheard-of volumes of domination and control were explored and tested. They were schools in which the unheard-of readiness to commit cruelty in formerly ordinary human beings was trained. And they were swords held over the heads of those remaining on the other side of the barbed-wire fence, so that they would learn not only that their dissent would not be tolerated but also that their consent was not called for, and that pretty little depends on their choice between protest and acclaim. The camps were distillations of an essence diluted elsewhere, condensations of totalitarian domination and its corollary, the superfluity of man, in a pure form difficult or impossible to achieve elsewhere. The camps were patterns and blueprints for the totalitarian society, that modern dream of total order, domination and mastery run wild, cleansed of the last vestiges of that wayward and unpredictable human freedom, spontaneity and predictability that held it back. The camps were testing grounds for societies run as concentration camps.[4]

And all this was, Bauman suggests, 'precisely the kind of universe dreamed up and promised by the philosophers of Enlightenment, to be pursued by the despots whom they sought to enlighten'.[5]

---

4 Zygmunt Bauman (1995), *Life in Fragments: Essays in Postmodern Morality*, Oxford: Blackwell, p.201. See also his *Modernity and the Holocaust*, Ithaca: Cornell University Press, 1991.
5 Bauman, *Life in Fragments: Essays in Postmodern Morality*, Oxford: Blackwell, 1995, p.198.

Nazism was based on terror, as exemplified above all in the camps. Stalin's tyranny was no better than Hitler's, and the number of deaths at the hands of his regime in the Gulag and elsewhere was far greater even than in the Holocaust. And the Second World War, provoked by Nazi aggression, was waged with unprecedented ferocity, even when compared with the First World War. This was especially true on the Eastern Front. But the western, and particularly British, emphasis on blanket bombing of German cities was vile, and the use of the only two nuclear bombs to be used – so far – in warfare, in attacks on Hiroshima and Nagasaki, was morally appalling.

The period of the Cold War with the balance of terror and the strategy of mutually assured destruction (MAD), froze a particular balance of power for more than 40 years, and allowed cruel dictatorships to flourish, not only behind the 'Iron Curtain'. The Cold War effectively ensured that major conflicts did not break out between East and West (the Korean and Vietnam wars were the most serious outbreaks) at the cost of often savage dealing with dissent on both sides. The Cold War balance of terror seemed almost permanent until its sudden collapse, leaving a world with only one superpower. The Cold War was never remotely like Kant's project for perpetual peace. Conflicts between the two great blocs during the Cold War were often fought out in proxy in restricted arenas, such as Afghanistan. Terrorist groups were armed and trained, but kept on a relatively tight rein for fear of sparking a nuclear disaster.

After the Cold War, other horrors occurred, in an even less orderly world. With the break-up of the old Yugoslavia, internecine conflict with a strong religious dimension returned to the Balkans. In Palestine/Israel, strife and terror continued despite all efforts to find a satisfactory settlement. There was genocide in East Timor. Latin American military dictatorships often exercised reigns of terror, ardently supported by the government of the USA. One need only mention the 'disappeared' in Argentina whose bodies were thrown from aeroplanes into the sea, and the horrors of Pinochet's dictatorship in Chile.

How is it possible to speak of God after Auschwitz and the Gulag, after the Rwanda genocide, after East Timor, and the chaos that is Iraq today? How can we have theology in a time of terror? Certainly there must be a renewed awareness of the pervasiveness of sin. The old liberal optimism of the Enlightenment cannot survive in today's world. We need a more realistic theology, which takes sin seriously, and is not afraid to speak of the remedy for sin, of guilt and forgiveness, of reconciliation and of hope even in face of all these horrors.

Chapter 3

After the Cold War: The End
of Ideology?

The sudden collapse of the Soviet Union and the communist states of eastern Europe in the late 1980s seemed to many to be the end of one age and the beginning of another. The great ideologies that had dominated thought and public life for two centuries and more seemed to have imploded and destroyed themselves. Was it that one ideology had triumphed? Or was it perchance that the Christianity that had been for much of the time excluded from the public forum by aggressively secular forces would return triumphantly to a place close to the seat of power? How was one to interpret and respond to the new situation, with all its opportunities and challenges?

The Re-evangelization of Europe?

There were those who saw Christianity as the major agent of the downfall of the Soviet empire, and now believed that there was an opportunity for Christianity, and specifically Roman Catholic Christianity, to play a leading role in Europe once again, filling the 'spiritual void' that had been left behind by Communism and other secular ideologies. If the wounds of the past were to be healed and the place of Christianity to be reaffirmed, there must, it was argued, be a 're-evangelization' of a Europe that had become largely pagan as a consequence of the atheistic indoctrination of the communist years, and the relentless process of secularization in most of the western countries.

The Polish Pope, John Paul II, celebrated in his encyclical *Centesimus Annus* what he saw as the triumph of the Christian Church and the forces of decency in the remarkable events of 1989, in which he himself had played no little role.[1] The sudden and largely unexpected collapse of the Soviet Union and the communist regimes of eastern Europe came in part, the Pope suggested, because working people 'forswore the ideology which presumed to speak in their name'. A whole vast political order in Europe

---

1   John Paul II (1991), *Centesimus Annus* (Encyclical Letter), London: CTS.

had been 'overcome by the non-violent commitment of people who, while always refusing to yield to the force of power, succeeded time after time in finding effective ways of bearing witness to the truth'. The opposition to Communism had been generated in 'the spiritual void brought about by atheism' and by politics becoming a 'secular religion' which gradually betrayed its inadequacies and its potentiality for evil on a gigantic scale.[2] The great political ideologies which had arisen after the Enlightenment had been shown to be ultimately destructive of basic human values and human dignity; the call was now to return to the faith that had in the twentieth century exposed the frailties, falsehoods and dangers of Marxist socialism and, earlier on, of Nazism.

The end of the Cold War, the Pope obviously believed and hoped, would usher in a return to religion, inaugurating a more humane, non-violent and Christian age when human dignity and proper solidarity would be consistently affirmed. The Church and the Christian faith should once again be at the heart of things. Before he became Pope, Karol Wojtyla had predicted with immense confidence the collapse of Communism, leaving behind a vacuum which could be filled only by a recovery of Christianity. As Pope he had the vision of a unified and re-Christianized Europe stretching from the Atlantic to the Urals, which would be once again the heart of the Christian world. Already in 1982 he had delivered, in Compostela, a 'Declaration to Europe' calling for the 're-evangelization of Europe', a kind of restoration of the old Christendom. He then proclaimed:

> It can be said that the European identity is not understandable without Christianity and it is precisely in Christianity that are found those common roots by which the continent has seen its civilization mature: its culture, its dynamism, its activity, its capacity for constructive expansion in other continents as well: in a word all that makes its glory. And truly still, the soul of Europe remains united because, beyond its common origin, it has similar Christian and human values, such as those of the dignity of the human person, a deep sense of justice and of liberty, of industry and a spirit of initiative, of love for the family, of respect for life, of tolerance with the desire for co-operation and peace, which are notes which characterise it.[3]

For long Europe has been bitterly and destructively divided by secular, atheistic and materialistic ideologies, especially Nazism and Communism. Now the Pope called Europe to

> *Find yourself again. Be yourself.* Discover your origins, revive your roots. Return to those authentic values which made your history a glorious one and your present

---

2   *Centesimus Annus*, pp.17–19.
3   *L'Observatore Romano*, weekly English edn, 29 November 1982, p.6.

so beneficial. You can still be the guiding light of civilization and the stimulus of progress for the world.[4]

The Pope's was not the only voice proclaiming the end of the old ideological systems and the totalitarian regimes in which they had sought expression. Others too longed for the restoration of a 'Christian Europe'. But the Pope was to be disappointed that in the aftermath of 1989 there was no very remarkable resurgence of Christianity, starting in Europe. Indeed, in some contexts, Christianity had survived more vigorously under persecution than when the persecution was no more. And the places where there has been a major revival of Christian practice have been by and large countries where there is a dangerous alliance between religion and chauvinistic nationalism.

The Pope clearly did not accept that the march of secularism was irresistible, any more than the coming of the Thousand Year Reich or the classless society had been inevitable. This was, he taught, the moment when Europe could reaffirm its ancient Christian heritage and 'come home', after the long secular search for the perfect society which had shown itself to be more than futile, but profoundly damaging to human dignity and human hopes. Like Hilaire Belloc, with his slogan, 'Europe is the Faith and the Faith is Europe', John Paul II was in fact affirming that the Roman Catholic Church is the soul, the vital principle, the continuity of Europe.[5]

The tone of Belloc and of John Paul II is triumphalistic. The Church is apparently without spot or wrinkle. There appears to be nothing in the history of Christian Europe of which modern Christians should be penitent. That history is 'glorious', and the present is 'beneficial'. Even the imperial expansion of Europe seems to be affirmed without question: 'its capacity for constructive expansion in other continents as well' is commemorated without penitence. Europe, it appears, has brought enlightenment, culture, virtue and faith to the rest of the world. There is no mention of the slave trade, of genocide, of ruthless exploitation, of cultural and religious arrogance on the part of Christian Europe. There is no call for repentance.

The hope that, with the collapse of the communist regimes and the end of the Cold War, Christianity would emerge strong and vindicated was not to be fulfilled. Except in some of the mainly Orthodox countries where Christianity had an implicit alliance with national chauvinism against an imposed communist dictatorship, the Church did not emerge from the Cold War stronger than before. Even in countries of Eastern Europe where the Church had provided virtually the only base for protest and the search for a more open future, the initial euphoria quickly faded. The majority of the

---

4   *L'Observatore Romano*, weekly English edn, 29 November 1982, p.6.
5   Hilaire Belloc (1962), *Europe and the Faith*, London: Burns and Oates, p.168.

people, it seemed, had been permanently alienated from the Christian faith
in and by the decades of atheistic indoctrination.

History is Finished!

A very distinctive, but typically western view of the triumph of one ideology
and of the secular in the aftermath of the Cold War was presented in 1993
by Francis Fukuyama, now a prominent adviser on foreign policy to
President Bush, and one who articulates an influential and still widespread
mindset, particularly in the United States. In his *The End of History and the
Last Man*, Fukuyama reflected, reinforced and commented on the euphoric
Zeitgeist of many in the West in the aftermath of the collapse of the
communist regimes of Eastern Europe.[6] He saw the events of 1989 as an
unqualified victory at every level for the West, rather as the Pope saw it as
a triumph for Christianity. The year 1989 was, Fukuyama suggested, the
definitive end of ideological conflict; liberal democracy with the free market
as its central institution had triumphed. There was now no alternative, and
it was no longer possible or desirable to carry out a throughgoing critique
of the now triumphant liberal democracy. 'We may be witnessing,'
Fukuyama suggested, 'the end of history as such: that is, the end point of
mankind's ideological evolution and the universalization of Western liberal
democracy as the final form of human government.'[7] And as he developed
his argument, the possibility of this generation standing at the End of
History became regarded as a certainty.

The end of history for Fukuyama, is more than just a turning point in
the human story. It is very much a Judaeo-Christian notion. It means that
history has reached its goal, its culmination. At the end of history,
Fukuyama writes astonishingly that 'the present form of social and political
organization is *completely satisfying* to human beings in their most essential
characteristics'.[8] Fukuyama also appears to believe, along with Kojève, that
'The end of history must also mean the end of wars and bloody revolutions.
Agreeing on ends, men would have no large causes for which to fight.'[9] This
is ironic as we stand in the confusing and bloody aftermath of a
controversial war in Iraq! History, in the sense of ideological debates about
alternative views of society and human flourishing, is at an end, argues
Fukuyama. All that is left is engineering and adjustment, fine-tuning heaven,
as it were. The possibility that religion might, in the twilight of ideology,

6   Francis Fukuyama (1993), *The End of History and the Last Man*, New York: Avon Books.
7   Francis Fukuyama (1989), 'The End of History', *The National Interest*, **16** (summer) p.4.
8   Fukuyama, *The End of History and the Last Man*, p.136; my italics.
9   Fukuyama, *The End of History and the Last Man*, p.311.

still sustain utopias and social vision is simply ruled out of court without question.

The end of history in the sense of the goal of history, is for Fukuyama unambiguously *secular*. Following Hegel, Fukuyama sees Christianity, particularly in its Protestant version, as having in the past played a great part in the evolution of history towards its end, and in defining that end. And religion, presumably for him meaning largely Christianity, may continue to play a part, but only in the private sphere. Inasmuch as this involves nurturing and sustaining community and implanting the civic virtues, religion may still be indirectly important for the general welfare of the civil community, but never again may it play its old magisterial role. Without religion, Fukuyama writes, basic forms of solidarity and cooperation are undercut. 'Families don't really work,' he argues, 'if they are based on liberal principles, that is, if their members regard them as they would a joint stock company, formed for their utility rather than being based on ties of duty and love' and 'On the level of the largest association, the country itself, liberal principles can be destructive of the highest forms of patriotism which are necessary for the very survival of the community.'[10] As Bauckham points out, Fukuyama seems to believe that modern liberalism, despite being definitive of 'the end of history', depends on pre-liberal and religiously rooted values, attitudes and ethics which it actually persistently corrodes.[11]

The end of history, Fukuyama believes, is thus also the end of religion as a significant player in the public square. In this he differs from most of his colleagues and allies in the American neoconservative movement. Public religion, for Fukuyama, essentially belongs to an earlier stage of development, and if it survives in lively form in the public domain it becomes divisive and an obstacle to progress.[12] 'If politics is based on something like religion,' he writes, 'there will never be any civil peace because people cannot agree on fundamental religious values.'[13] Apparently it is easier to achieve a consensus on secular values and secular goals. Religion in all its forms seems, according to Fukuyama, to resist modernity and progress. None the less, for Fukuyama, 'modern democracy is a secularized version of the Christian doctrine of universal human equality'.

---

10   Fukuyama, *The End of History and the Last Man*, pp.324–5. On this point see Richard Bauckham's essay, 'Freedom in the Crisis of Modernity', in Andrew Morton and William Storrar (2004), *Public Theology for the 21st Century*, London: Continuum, pp.77–94.

11   Richard Bauckham, 'Freedom in the Crisis of Modernity', p.83.

12   I am reminded at this point of the excesses of the modernization theories of the 1960s. Everything, including religion, was to be 'modernized' in the image of western societies. There is a tale which may be true, that the great scholar of religions, Wilfred Cantwell Smith, was offered a large sum by a development agency if he would act as a consultant on the elimination of religion in India, as an obstacle to modernization!

13   Francis Fukuyama (2002), 'Their Target: The Modern World', *Newsweek*, February, p.56.

But liberal democracy is more than an offshoot of Christianity; it now has universal reference and value, and has become detached from its Christian roots. And it is against modernity and the universal value of liberal democracy that we are now seeing on the part of major religious groups, he writes, '*a desperate backlash against the modern world*',[14] which is often mistakenly presented as opposition to aggressive western Christianity. He seems quite insensitive to the immense and influential 'backlash against the modern world' on the part of the American religious Right.

Fukuyama's book should perhaps count as a kind of liberal democratic apocalyptic. There is a simple dualism between good and evil. There has been a holy war, which is expected to be the last great battle: how ironic that sounds today! Fukuyama's cataclysmic war to end war has resulted, he believes, in the victory of the secular saints over the powers of religious darkness. But in this new Jerusalem there is nothing left to hope for. Indeed hope has become redundant, even seditious, in this 'best of all possible worlds'.

Reading Fukuyama we may become aware of the reasons why many in the third world, especially Muslims, see secular liberal democracy as a militant, specifically Christian and religious project which is deeply hostile to Islam and would allow it to survive only if confined to the private sphere.[15] Religion today may indeed offer totalitarian and oppressive systems of thought and action which are at least as frightening as the old ideological systems of the twentieth century. But is it perhaps also the case that only religion may today fuel and guide a renewed 'history', giving hope that a society of justice and of peace may be established upon earth, affirming that change is possible?

Ideology after 9/11

Some saw the end of ideology as manifested most directly in the efforts to understand and respond to the horrors of 9/11, allied with the decline of religion as a significant player in the public sphere. For many people, Christians and others, the Pope had been right in suggesting that we had come to the 'End of Ideology', so confidently, and prematurely proclaimed by Daniel Bell in the 1950s. For some, ideology was a kind of surrogate religion; for others it was a series of systems of thought which had shown themselves both incapable of discerning 'the signs of the times' and positively harmful to human flourishing.

John Gray, the LSE philosopher, wrote in the aftermath of 9/11:

---

14   Fukuyama, *Newsweek*, p.54; my italics.
15   It is interesting that Salman Rushdie has called for the 'privatization' of Islam.

'Al-Qaeda did more than demolish a familiar landmark and kill thousands of civilians. It shattered an entire view of the world.' He continued:

> If progressives are aghast at the turn of events, they are not alone. The western intelligentsia as a whole is more confused and marginal than it has been for generations. In the past Marx, Keynes, Dewey, Popper or Hayek gave illumination. None of these thinkers has anything of interest to say about the circumstances we face today. All of them subscribed to the Enlightenment faith that as societies became more modern, they became more alike, accepting the same secular values and the same view of the world. That faith was always questionable. Today it is incredible. If now we reach to our shelves for books that can help us to understand what happened on 11 September, we find almost nothing.[16]

I think John Gray is largely right in this. In past decades Christians struggled with Marxism and neoconservatism, and Keynsian economics. The encounter with Marxism after the Second World War was particularly significant. In Marx's thought there were resonances of the Bible, and indeed of the gospel, especially understanding salvation as the overcoming of alienation and the hope of a new heaven and earth, so dramatically developed by the heretical Marxist, Ernst Bloch. The Marxist–Christian dialogue deeply influenced Liberation Theology, articulating and supporting its passion for justice, its confidence in the historical process and its emphasis on structural sin. Yet all the while compelling evidence was accumulating not only that things under Stalin in the Soviet Union and Eastern Europe had gone dramatically wrong, but that the Gulag was as awful a structural evil as the Holocaust. Disillusion with the Marxist project spread fast, as people realized it was not in practice good news, but the very opposite. Yet the Marxist variant of the Enlightenment critique of religion to the effect that it was the opium of the people that made the masses resigned to their lot because they lived in a fantasy world continued to reinforce the general belief in the West that religion was a largely malign relic of the past, like the state in Marxist theory doomed to wither away. But to many today it is Marxism which seems to be the fantasy which obscures rather than revealing reality, and gives little help in understanding the world in which we now live.

With the end of ideology for much of the world the winds have gone out of the sails of utopia, and as a consequence the ideologies that claimed to be in some sense good news, able to interpret and assess today through the lens of hope for a better tomorrow, have all but disintegrated. Radical theology is left looking for new dialogue partners that operate in similar ground to that of theology. The collapse of revolutionary Marxism as an

---

16 John Gray (2002), 'Why terrorism is unbeatable', *The New Statesman*, 25 February, p.50.

interpretative framework has left democratic socialism in most places to be either a matter of tinkering or as a world-view searching for its soul and for policies to express a diffuse orientation to life, at its worst disguising rather than illuminating what is in fact going on. The dreary procession we have seen in Britain through 'stakeholding', the 'Third Way', and multitudinous focus groups suggests that democratic socialism has lost its way. And liberal democracy has been shown in Britain and the United States, and many other democracies as well, as a system which can be manipulated by irresponsible forces, and where wealth rather than debate wins the day.

Realism in international relations, in which the American theologian Reinhold Niebuhr was a distinguished figure, engaged with the ambiguities of power, but now seems profoundly confused as to how to react to a post-Cold War situation in which the traditional restraints of balance of power no longer seem applicable, and key players are not states or nations but diffuse yet coordinated global groupings like al-Qaeda or, to borrow Huntington's tricky term, 'civilizations'. Since the Peace of Westphalia, world politics has been dominated by relations between states and balances of power. With the rise of terrorism and terrorist groups which are not controlled or managed by any state or group of states we are in a radically new ballgame, in which the goals 'are less political than apocalyptic',[17] and the rules are far from clear. In addition, as Bernard Lewis has forcefully argued, Muslims commonly see themselves as belonging primarily to a religion subdivided into nations, rather like some understandings of the old Christendom.[18] But, above all, we have an almost unprecedented situation, with one superpower, the United States, whose will and whose actions seem almost beyond question or challenge. And almost universally liberal democracy is said to be essentially secular, or at lest demanding a clear barrier between the spheres of politics and those of religion.

As we have seen, in the West there has been, especially among intellectuals, an increasing suspicion of religion, combined with a strange confidence that religion is rapidly declining and is indeed on the way to public oblivion. Sometimes these secular intellectuals give the impression of dancing on the grave of religion. But others believe that religion is far from dead, and indeed in some places is experiencing a resurrection. In the rest of the world, and indeed in parts of the West as well, there has been in recent times what Gilles Kepel has called 'la revanche de Dieu'.[19] Religion

---

17   Michael Ignatieff (2003), 'The Lesser Evil: Political Ethics in an Age of Terror', Gifford Lectures in the University of Edinburgh, lecture 5 (typescript).

18   Bernard Lewis (2003a), *The Crisis of Islam: Holy War and Unholy Terror*, London: Orion, p.xix.

19   Gilles Kepel (1994), *Revenge of God: The Resurgence of Islam, Christianity and Judaism in the Modern World*, University Park, PA: Pennsylvania State University Press, p.2.

in most of the world is not disintegrating; to the contrary, the major religious systems are flourishing, and growing in confidence and in numbers.

It is impossible responsibly either to applaud or to deplore such a development. It is full of actualities and possibilities of good and of evil. But any considered response should take into account the reality of what is happening rather than what the observer wishes were happening.

Hope and Social Critique

What much of the world sees today is not the end of history but the replacement of the restraints and constraints of the old balance of power, and especially the balance of terror of the Cold War times, with a single superpower, and the almost unchallengeable hegemony of the West.

In reality, we have a volatile 'New World Disorder', which is radically different from the old orders, and in which styles of thought and theology which provided illumination in the past seem powerless to understand. Ironically Fukuyama predicted that the consequence of 1989 would be not only the end of ideology, but also the end of religion as a significant player in the public arena. He could not have been more wrong.

If we indeed stand at the end of history, as Francis Fukuyama proclaims, there is nothing left to hope for. We have arrived. The absolute moment is now. We confront with puzzled feelings what Lyotard calls 'the end of hopes (modernity's hell)'.[20] The triumph of liberal democracy means that there is nothing further to strive for, no possibility of fundamental criticism of our consumerist society. All that is left is to fine-tune heaven. 'Liberal democracy,' writes Fukuyama, 'is the only legitimate ideology left in the world.'[21] The hopes of the past have turned sour, or shown themselves to be poisonous. We are better off without them. 'We can smooth off the rough edges of the present and call it Zion.'[22] And so a New World Order is proclaimed, to freeze and protect the absolute moment, the end of history, at which we have arrived.

My reading of Fukuyama suggests that the sustaining of social hope in today's world now devolves mainly upon organized religion in the absence of convincing and coherent ideological systems of social criticism and change. Not only is the secular far less triumphant in today's world than we

---

20 J.-F. Lyotard (1997), *Postmodern Fables*, Minneapolis: University of Minnesota Press, p.100, cited in R. Bauckham and T. Hart (eds) (1997), *Hope Against Hope*, London: Darton, Longman and Todd, p.25.

21 Francis Fukuyama (1990), *The Guardian*, 17 Sept.

22 Lee Griffith (2002), *The War on Terrorism and the Terror of God*, Grand Rapids: Eerdmans, p.169.

used to think, but in some ways the secular mindset blinds people to recognizing the significance and continuing power of religion, or taking a constructive part in dialogues with representatives of the resurgent world religions. The next chapter will examine the extraordinary resurgence of religion around the world that secular thinkers like Francis Fukuyama and many other secular theorists find hard to understand and take into account.

Chapter 4

The Public Voice of Resurgent Religion

Resurgence and Discord

Almost all around the world, with the striking exception of western Europe, religion in a multitude of forms, from what Peter Berger calls 'furious religion' to transcendental meditation, is powerfully resurgent. There are a variety of interpretations of this development. Some see religion in this generation as rushing in to fill the vacuum left by 'the end of ideology'. This is perhaps true of the United States more markedly even than the Middle East and the southern hemisphere, where to some extent societies were immune to the Enlightenment, and were seldom as dominated by secular ideologies as the West. Religion there has always been a major player in the public arena. Those, on the other hand, who agree with Fukuyama that we stand at the end of history tend to see the worldwide resurgence of religion as a wild and desperate protest against the modern world and all modernity stands for. For some, resurgent religion is the only way of opposing American Empire and its supportive ideologies. Others again see liberal democracy, especially as exemplified in the United States, as itself offering a vacuum of values under a thin veneer of Christianity, in which immorality, faithlessness and irreligion flourish without restraint. Sexual torture and degradation in Abu Ghraib prison, and other horrific incidents, confirm such opinions. And it is easy to argue that religion, meaning in this case right-wing conservative Christianity, has never been as influential in American politics as it is today in the presidency of George W. Bush.[1]

Huntington, in his argument in *The Clash of Civilizations and the Remaking of World Order* (1996),[2] draws on Gilles Kepel's fascinating and controversial analysis. Kepel argues that, since the 1970s, not only has there been a massive recrudescence of the great world faiths, but this has taken a new form:

---

1   For a vigorous treatment of American evangelical religion and its political impact today, see Michael Northcott (2004), *An Angel Directs the Storm: Apocalyptic Religion and American Empire*, London: Tauris.
2   Samuel P. Huntington (1996), *The Clash of Civilizations and the Remaking of World Order*, New York: Touchstone.

A new religious approach took shape, aimed no longer at adapting to secular values but at recovering a sacred foundation for the organization of society – by changing society if necessary. Expressed in a multitude of ways, this approach advocated moving on from a modernism that had failed, attributing its setbacks and dead ends to separation from God. The theme was no longer *aggiornamento* but a 'second evangelization of Europe': the aim was no longer to modernize Islam but to 'Islamize modernity'.[3]

scm ?

All the varied manifestations of this new approach reject western secularism and seek in their holy books and in their traditions of faith resources to understand what is happening in the world, and provide guidelines for behaviour. Thus the theological debate within particular religious systems, and dialogue between religions assume a vast importance, for their fruits may do great good or wreak havoc with the social order. These religious discussions are far more important than the self-consciously secular discussions in the western public forum, with John Rawls and his like as the gatekeepers.

This scenario that Huntington and Kepel depict makes a clash, or clashes, of civilizations highly likely, if not inevitable. And Huntington is now quite specific: we are at the beginning of the era of what he calls 'Muslim wars'. These Muslim wars have replaced the Cold War as the principal form of international conflict.[4] He points to the fact that, in the 1990s, there was a large number of conflicts between Muslims and non-Muslims around the world, most of the non-Muslims being in some form or other Christians. In typically western secular fashion, he declares that 'The causes of contemporary Muslims wars lie in politics, not seventh century religious doctrines', and are a response to modernization and globalization, and reflect 'a great sense of grievance, resentment, envy and hostility toward the West and its wealth, power and culture.'[5] And 11 September 2001 demonstrated that 'the makings of a general clash of civilizations exist'.[6]

The point at which we must part company with Huntington is the place of religion and theology in the present development of a resurgent, confident and often aggressive Islam. It is true that there is a deep sense of grievance among many Muslims and it is not hard to appreciate at least some of the roots of this. There are certainly economic and political foundations for Muslim fears and anger, but most Muslims would affirm that the single most important factor for them is Muslim faith, as variously interpreted. For Christians, Jews and Muslims alike, there is that in theology

---

3   Gilles Kepel (1994), *Revenge of God: The Resurgence of Islam, Christianity and Judaism in the Modern World*, Oxford: Polity, p.2.

4   Samuel P. Huntington, 'The Age of Muslim Wars', *Newsweek*, Dec. 2001–Feb. 2002, p.8.

5   Huntington, 'The Age of Muslim Wars', p.9.

6   Huntington, 'The Age of Muslim Wars', p.13.

and authoritative sacred writings which may incite, or discipline, surges of anger and encourage the faithful either to hit back, remorselessly seeking vengeance and vindication, or with quiet faithfulness and even resignation leave the issue in the hands of God. The debates about theology and holy books, and about apocalyptic are thus important, for they can deeply influence behaviour for good or ill, and they are arguably more influential in the politics and economics of the world today than any secular ideology or theory.

Competing Religions

What we face today, for better or for worse, is a world dominated by diverse religions, competing political theologies and radically different understandings of God and the world, of what faith means, and of the kind of practice which is appropriate for believers. The diversity, conflict and suspicion is both within and between these competing and very different religious traditions. Especially after 9/11 it is quite impossible to sustain the bland assumption that religion as such, or at least most religion, is almost by definition 'a good thing'. We have all now experienced religion as justifying and motivating radical evil.

The world religions on the whole share a deep suspicion of modern western secularism, although to be sure some expressions of Christianity have sought an accommodation with secularism, or have even, like Dietrich Bonhoeffer or Harvey Cox, felt that as Christians they should celebrate secularism and the new possibilities for faith that it offers. The encounter over recent centuries of Christianity and Judaism with secularism may have lessons, positive and negative, to teach other religions which have more recently engaged with secularism. But secularism as such is widely regarded outside the West as effectively another religious system, or a quasi-religious outcome of Christianity.

Islam, Hinduism, Christianity, even Buddhism have shown themselves frequently to be aggressive, intolerant and arrogant. Modern history is full of conflicts, atrocities and crimes which have been at least in part religiously motivated. One thinks of ethnic cleansing in Bosnia, the continuing spiral of violence in Israel and Palestine, the bitter communal conflicts between Hindu and Muslim in India, to say nothing of Northern Ireland, or the long agony of Afghanistan. Even if some of these conflicts can be seen as primarily political or economic, we must not dodge the fact that they are commonly seen by those at the eye of the storm as essentially religious. And at this point it is worth remembering that certain forms of secularism, such as Communism and Nazism, have wrought in the twentieth century at least as much evil as any explicitly religious system.

Religion can be, and often is, a very evil thing, but modern attempts to eliminate religion, say in the Soviet Union, not only were markedly unsuccessful, but in many ways appear to have backfired. Religion seems not only to survive, but often to flourish, under persecution of one sort or another: the old saying that the blood of the martyrs is the seed of the church has much truth in it. We have to learn how to cope constructively with the modern manifestations of religion, in all their moral ambiguity and their moral magnificence.

There is not nearly enough real and realistic dialogue between religions, and many religions are at pains to silence internal critical and questioning voices. We need, for example, more prominent Muslim voices questioning the view of Islam and the eschatology of al-Qaeda and the Taliban. We need more Jewish voices within Israel challenging Sharon's policy on Palestine; and more Christian and Muslim Palestinians questioning whether suicide bombers are indeed martyrs. We need more people within the 'Christian' West challenging our complacency and urging us to listen attentively to the view from the other side. In the real world, things are never black and white, but always in shades of grey. And if there is to be real dialogue between religions about the state of the world and what should be done, the conversation has to be attentive, serious, engaging with the subtext as well as the text, attempting strenuously to understand the other. And religious believers should be peculiarly qualified to enter sympathetically and with understanding into religious positions, attitudes and practices that they do not themselves share. But it is sadly only too common for religious people to affirm arrogantly that they possess the whole truth, and to show in consequence huge resistance to learning from those of other faiths, or of none.

In all the great religions there are major internal conflicts, and varying attitudes to modernity and post-modernity. Christian theology, for example, is perhaps in a special position to share the 'successes' and the 'failures' in its experience of encounter with modernity with the other world faiths in an open dialogue, the kind of dialogue which is only possible between believers, or at least those who are critically appreciative of religion. Christian responses to the end of 'Christendom' may suggest creative possibilities to some Muslims. And these same Muslims may suggest fairly enough that Christianity in some of its forms has capitulated too easily to the Enlightenment.

All the resurgent religions have a public voice which they hope to make powerfully heard throughout the world through actions, through the modern mass media and through personal contacts and conversations. These voices are often strident, angry and threatening. Almost always they claim to be rooted in fundamental theological truths, and regard the theological expression as indispensable. In controversy slogans are hurled around and there is seldom a meeting of minds, and agreement, or a serious listening to the other side's opinions. They operate in a public sphere that is more an arena than a forum, where consensus is rarely the goal, but the discourse is directed largely at shaming one's opponents, and recruiting disciples and supporters from among the audience. There is a serious problem in seeing how religious discourse may be constructive and unifying rather than destructive and divisive. Almost the only thing that most of the public and conflicting voices of religion have in common today is a conviction that theology matters, that theology is a, or the, bearer of truth and that theology should have a central place in public debate.

In such a confusing and conflictual situation, a number of ways forward have been presented, and need to be examined. I look first at Hans Küng's 'Global Ethics' project.

Global Ethics?

If we are to look to the religions, in all their confusing diversity, for help in responding to the present global crisis and the 'war on terror', a possible way forward might be the 'Global Ethics' developed by the senior German theologian, Hans Küng, with the support of a galaxy of world public figures. Küng starts with some stirring slogans: 'No survival without a world ethic. No world peace without peace between the religions. No peace between the religions without dialogue between the religions'.[7] He then moves towards 'Declarations' endorsed by prominent figures, most notably the 'Declaration toward a Global Ethic' promulgated by the Parliament of World Religions in 1993, and the 'Universal Declaration of Human Responsibilities' approved by an international group of retired statesmen chaired by Helmut Schmidt in 1997.[8] Küng explains the origins of his project thus:

> It has become increasingly clear to me in recent years that the one world in which we live has a chance of survival only if there is no longer in it any room for spheres of differing, contradictory and even antagonistic ethics. This one world needs one basic ethic. This one world society certainly does not need a unitary religion and a unitary ideology, but it does need some norms, values, ideals and goals to bring it together and to be binding on it.[9]

The modern world, and democracy in particular, Küng argues, needs a basic consensus about morals. There are surely shades here of Rawls' 'overlapping

---

7   Hans Küng (1991), *Global Responsibility: In Search of a New World Ethic*, London: SCM, p.xv.

8   Hans Küng and Helmut Schmidt (1998), *A Global Ethic and Global Responsibilities: Two Declarations*, London: SCM Press.

9   Küng, *Global Responsibility*, p.xvi.

consensus' projected onto the world stage.[10] Otherwise, Küng suggests, all we have are irreconcilable antinomies at every turn, and serious ethical conversation breaks down. We are then left simply with the law of the jungle.

For Küng, the core of the morality that is common to all religions is simply 'do not kill, do not steal, do not lie, do not commit sexual immorality'.[11] On this foundation a global ethic is developed, which is believed to complement and correct the modern emphasis on rights with an emphasis on duties or responsibilities. Both documents claim to present a 'fundamental consensus on binding values', which is endorsed by 'women and men who have embraced the precepts and practices of the world's religions'. But neither Declaration mentions God – apparently at the insistence of the Buddhist participants in the discussion and formulation of the Declarations.

It is, Küng suggests, hard to separate religion and ethics; pragmatically a 'Godless morality' would hardly commend itself to the millions of religious believers in the world, and all the great world religions affirm that there is an organic relation between faith and practice. Religion thus remains a possible or necessary foundation for ethics, and a global ethics can only be founded on the great world religions, which have, he argues, a great amount of moral belief in common. And yet this global ethic must also be formulated in such a way that 'philosophers too, like agnostics and atheists, can make it their own, even if they do not share a possible transcendent ground for such a concrete form'.[12] Küng continues:

> To be specific, anyone in the prophetic tradition who truly believes in God should in practice be concerned with human wellbeing. Hence the twofold Jewish commandment to love God and one's neighbour and its radicalization (to the point of loving one's enemy) in Jesus' Sermon on the Mount, along with the incessant demand of the Qur'an for justice, truth and good works. But the Buddhist doctrine of the overcoming of human suffering should also be mentioned here, along with the Hindu striving to fulfil 'dharma' and Confucius' requirement to preserve the cosmic order and thus the *humanum*. In all these instances human wellbeing and dignity as the basic principle and goal of human ethics is brought out with unconditional authority – in a way that only the religions can and may do it. That means human life, integrity, freedom and solidarity in quite specific instances. Human dignity, human freedom and human rights can thus not only be stated in positivistic terms, but also given a basis in an ultimate depth, a religious basis.[13]

---

10   Rawls himself tries this in his *The Law of Peoples with 'The Idea of Public Reason Revisited'*, Cambridge, MA: Harvard University Press, 1999.

11   This section is indebted to Oliver O'Donovan's incisive comments in his review in *Studies in Christian Ethics*, **13** (1), 2000, pp.122–1128.

12   Küng (1997), *A Global Ethic for Global Politics and Economics*, London: SCM Press, p.105.

13   Küng, *Global Responsibility*, p.56.

Within this framework, Küng launches an ambitious attempt to 'rediscover and reassess ethics in politics and economics', and to present a realistic vision of the future as a more peaceful, just and humane world. His book starts with two chapters on politics and economics, using Kissinger, Richelieu, Bismark, Woodrow Wilson and Hans Morgenthau as representatives of varying traditions of theory and practice. A further two chapters discuss in a broad-brush way the possibility of an ethical politics in which a 'global ethics' is at the heart, insisting that every human being must be treated humanely and that we should do to others what we wish done to us. The political section concludes with a chapter on world peace and the role of religion in peacemaking, with examples and warnings from Yugoslavia and elsewhere. The economics section likewise covers a lot of ground, from the crisis of the welfare state to the principles of business ethics, by way of discussion of neocapitalism, the market economy, sustainable development, and other matters.

Küng's book as a whole is benign, well-intentioned and often interesting, but at key points it is remarkably vague, and sometimes descends into sloganizing. Much of it is moralizing rather than rigorous reflection on ethical issues and, when it turns to deal with really complex developments such as the Rwanda genocide, or the break-up of Yugoslavia, it is clear that good intentions and vague moral principles are not enough.

It is easy to forget that Küng is in fact a distinguished theologian, for references to the rich and complex tradition of theological reflection on politics and economics are remarkably sparse and sometimes dismissive. He is no Reinhold Niebuhr, advising politicians and statesmen on the ironies, ambiguities and dilemmas of public life, seeking to discern 'the signs of the times' in a fallen, sinful world, and wrestling with the ambiguities, ironies and tragedies of public life. Nor is Küng a liberation theologian, wrestling with the realities of oppression and exploitation. Rather he is convinced that the world religions, because they have so much in common, are capable of being a powerful force for good in politics and economics in today's global village. And this is laudable and important. But the really interesting and difficult questions such as why the world religions find it so hard to work together beyond the pronouncement of pious generalities and ethical platitudes, and why religion is so often at the root of oppression, injustice and violence, and what can be done about these things, are hardly addressed. Deep-seated differences between religions, and within religions, about theology and ethics are passed over almost without a mention.

Küng suggests that there is a 'middle way between real politics and ideal politics', which is what Max Weber called an ethic of responsibility. But he hardly goes any distance in spelling out what an ethic of responsibility would actually involve. Küng's global ethics seems hardly likely to be able to take the measure of events such as those that took place on and since

11 September 2001, religiously sanctioned terror and religiously sanctioned counter-terror.

Küng's project demonstrates that it is not hard to achieve broad agreement on ethical generalities. But the real problems arise, not so much at the level of general principle, but rather when one is attempting to resolve concrete and complex issues on the ground, where there are various views on what is at stake, conflicting interests involved, and no clear-cut and agreed resolution in sight. In such situations, in the muck and grime of the real world, agreement on general principles often falls apart.

Küng's global ethics is, according to Oliver O'Donovan, a 'Highest Common Factor ethic'. It is intended to help us to understand what is going on in the world better, and respond more effectively. But this it will not do, and cannot do, because 'it does not *transcend* the limitations of vision which the various traditions bring with them, but *compounds* them, excluding from common discussion those things which only one tradition, or a few, have come to know. Yet this weakness is precisely its strength as a legitimating ideology, for it offers the promise of global agreement at the most truistic and least reflective level without promoting critical reflection on the *fait accompli* of globalisation'.[14]

But Küng's global ethics project does at least point to the need for serious and honest dialogue between theologians and leaders of the world's great faiths. Perhaps this might go some way towards avoiding the *Clash of Civilizations* that Samuel Huntington predicts.[15] Huntington sees conflict between religiously based civilizations as almost inevitable in the post-Cold War era: 'Muslim wars,' he writes, 'have replaced the cold war as the principal form of international conflict.'[16] While he sees the causes of conflict in Muslim wars as political rather than theological, the alignments are religiously defined and it is clear that many Muslims interpret these conflicts primarily in theological terms, or at least with recourse to religious symbols. There is therefore a major place for serious and honest inter-religious dialogue, as well as for debate within Islam. And, in this debate, Christians may offer lessons that have been learned from the experience of Christianity with the complex and enticing notion of Christendom.

A Common Morality?

In a way Küng's global ethics project is a modern, and rather simple,

---

14   See Oliver O'Donovan's review in *Studies in Christian Ethics*, **13** (1), 2000, p.125.
15   Samuel P. Huntington (1997), *The Clash of Civilizations and the Remaking of World Order*, New York: Touchstone.
16   Samuel P. Huntington (2001), 'The Age of Muslim Wars', *Newsweek*, December 2001–February 2002, p.8.

development of the ancient idea that there is a common morality which is shared by most or all human beings and is accessible to, and binding upon, all rational beings independent of their religious belief, or lack of it. This position takes two principal forms today. The first suggests that, in western societies, Christian values have penetrated so deeply into the culture that a major task for the churches and theology is to affirm and strengthen these implanted moral values, which at heart are Christian, but may well be supported by those of many faiths, or of none. Despite secularization, the decline in Christian practice and the increase in the number of adherents of other religions who live in Britain, Britain is still a basically Christian nation and culture, so the argument runs. The task is to affirm these values of decency and basic morality, on which there is already a widespread consensus.[17] Other world faiths, it is assumed, have implanted very similar ethical stances in the cultures they have shaped; in plural societies, as in the western democracies, the great faiths can work together to sustain and strengthen an ethical consensus which is quite similar to Küng's global ethics.

Allied to this kind of commitment to a common morality is frequently a conviction that, in speaking in the public forum, the church and theology, and religious people generally, should eschew distinctively Christian or religious language and perspectives, and speak 'the language of the world'. The American Jesuit, John Langan, has declared that 'In a pluralistic society it is both a tactical mistake and an error of principle to base controversial public policies on purely religious grounds.'[18] In commenting on a Church of England report that adopted Langan's approach, Professor Nigel Biggar perceptively says: 'Here the Church is permitted to speak only in confirmation, not in criticism; only to second, not to propose. The Church may proclaim more loudly the good the world already knows; but not the good that comes to the world as news.'[19]

Now it is obvious that in any community or society there is a need for some shared language of the good if we are to live together and cooperate with relative strangers. But this language is limited and circumscribed. We also need a richer, and necessarily more controversial, language of the good if we are to be able to handle complex issues effectively. And what if the assumptions that the operative common morality sustains are seriously mistaken, and need to be challenged?

The American Mennonite theologian, John Howard Yoder, acknowledges that 'There is the need in public life [not only in politics] for a common

---

17 See A.E. Harvie (2001), *By What Authority?*, London: SCM.
18 John Langan (1980), in *Commonweal*, 29 February, 1980, p.98.
19 Nigel Biggar (1987), 'Any News of What's Good for Society?', *Latimer Comment*, **24**, Oxford, p.3.

denominator language in order to collaborate with relative strangers in running the world despite our abiding differences.' But he was rather reluctant to spell out how this shared language is related to the gospel, whether it is separate and independent, and how, if at all, it relates to the call to discipleship. While Yoder recognized the need for some common language of morals, he argued that this common morality is limited and needs constantly to be challenged and enriched by insights from Christian discipleship. Christians need in discussion with non-Christians to decide what is the right thing to do. 'In ethics,' he writes, 'we have to act, and sometimes act together, by the nature of the issue. Scarce resources cannot be spent everywhere. Life will be taken or spared; we can't have it both ways.'[20] In such situations we cannot simply appeal to the Bible, to Christian doctrine or to a command of God without giving reasons. But sometimes through our ethics and our behaviour we have to witness to the truth of the gospel, the truth of our theology. Yoder was also deeply suspicious of claims that natural law on its own can provide an adequate 'neutral' structure for such decision-making discussions.

The other approach to common morality has a distinguished ancestry. It is natural law. This forms the backbone of Roman Catholic moral teaching to this day. Natural law is 'read off' the moral structure of the universe. It is understood as in a real sense God's law, but it is accessible to any rational being, independently of religious belief or its absence. It is universal, valid everywhere and binding on everyone. This account of natural law has been challenged by John Howard Yoder in a remarkable passage:

> The function of the notion of 'nature' in medieval Catholic thought was *not* the modern one of knowing how to talk with outsiders. ... The appeal to 'nature' was an instrument of *less* rather than *more* commonality with non-Christians ... The concern with 'nature' then bespoke not a growing readiness to converse with others in non-Christian language, but rather a growing conviction that the way Christians see reality is the way it really is. But the way to affirm our respect for others is to respect their particularity and learn their languages, not to project in their absence a claim that we see the truth of things with an authority unvitiated by our particularity.[21]

Most Protestant moral theology has also allocated a major place to natural law, but there has often been a sharp tension recognized between law and

20   Yoder's unpublished paper, 'Regarding Nature' (drafted and circulated in connection with a Notre Dame course on the Just War Tradition, 1994), Notre Dame Collection of John Yoder's writings, http://www.nd.edu/~theo/jhy/writings/philsystheo/nature.htm.

21   John Howard Yoder (1984), 'The Hermeneutics of Peoplehood: A Protestant Perspective', *The Priestly Kingdom: Social Ethics as Gospel*, Notre Dame, ID: University of Notre Dame Press, p.42.

gospel. Karl Barth, for instance, launched a frontal attack on the notion of natural law as part of his repudiation of natural theology. It was, he held, based on the frail foundation of fallen human reason, and denied the specificity of the divine command, while Stanley Hauerwas and his disciples reject any universalising ethic. And confidence in natural law as traditionally understood seems to be weakening even in the Roman Catholic Church. Social encyclicals, for instance, now commonly include substantial reflection on the circumstances of the day, attempt to 'discern the signs of the times' and adapt moral guidance to changing circumstances. Furthermore there has been an increasing use of biblical motifs alongside natural law arguments, as if to suggest that natural law reasoning has its limits, and requires supplementation or correction by more confessional language. Yet still the dominant view in the Roman Catholic Church is that, on public issues, the Church 'does not present proofs of faith, but gives arguments based on reason, which she considers valid and, therefore, acceptable also for those who do not believe'.[22]

Religious Reasons in the Public Forum

At this stage I want to focus briefly on the debate in the West, and particularly in the United States, about the conditions on which religious arguments and religious reasons might be legitimately admitted to the public forum. This debate is not only important in itself, but it has some perplexing features and ironies. In the first place, the way it is outlined and pursued reflects the rapid and radical secularization among liberal American intellectuals in the last few decades. We now have predominantly sceptical or agnostic intellectuals in a society in which, unlike Western Europe, most people profess religious belief, and religious observance continues to flourish exceedingly – some would say excessively. And these secular intellectuals, with the support of a series of court decisions on 'the wall of separation between church and state', have constituted themselves the gatekeepers of the public forum, determining which arguments, and on what conditions, may be entertained in public deliberation.

Their consensus is that only *rational* arguments which do not rely on any other source of wisdom than the human reason may be admitted. Rationality is often left rather loosely defined. And it is assumed, rather than demonstrated, that religious reasons and religious arguments are irrational and have no place in public discourse unless they can be translated without remainder into secular language, and meet modern secular standards of

---

22 Archbishop Giovanni Lasjolo, the Vatican's Secretary for Relations with States, in an interview in *La Stampa*, 3 Nov. 2004.

truth. Behind this there lies, of course, a host of assumptions about religion as something primitive which is doomed to disappear with the advance of enlightenment, and religion as a malign, divisive and threatening form of irrationality.

John Rawls is perhaps the most open and influential of the social theorists I have in mind at this point. It has been argued that Rawls has moved from a position where he regarded religion in all its forms as simply divisive, arbitrary and irrational, and thus to be excluded as far as possible from the public realm and confined to private life. Now his view seems to be slightly more sympathetic, or realistic, in relation to religion. In recent writings he seems to be saying that religious views may be admitted to the public forum provided they meet the commonly accepted criteria of public reasoning, and can be expressed in secular, non-religious terms. He instances the Roman Catholic understanding of natural law as just such a transposition of religious views into secular form to qualify them for admission to public debate.[23]

Furthermore Rawls, in developing the idea of what he calls the 'overlapping consensus' among 'reasonable comprehensive doctrines', locates public political reasoning in the *overlap* between these comprehensive world-views. In a democratic society, he argues, there will be a variety of reasonable world-views which however converge in supporting a common understanding of justice, and the fundamental principles of social order.

There are two important issues here. In the first place, how and who decides whether a comprehensive religious or other doctrine is 'reasonable', and thus worthy of being admitted to the public sphere? Is the introduction here of the criterion of reasonability a way of excluding from the discussion overconfident religious or ideological systems that wish to reshape the society, or which challenge the existing order of things, or indeed which ask fundamental critical questions? Such systems are often only too reasonable and intellectually coherent! But according to Rawls, the common religious 'zeal to embody the whole truth in politics is incompatible with an idea of public reason that belongs with democratic citizenship'.[24] Is this caveat about 'the whole religious truth' in fact an excuse for excluding some kinds of truth from politics? Is it possible that comprehensive positions which modern secular western intellectuals find peculiarly difficult to understand and appreciate are, on that ground, dismissed as unreasonable, almost out of intellectual laziness?

---

23   John Rawls (1999), *The Law of Peoples, with 'The Idea of Public Reason Revisited'*, Cambridge, MA: Harvard University Press, p.142: 'Political liberalism also admits … Catholic views of the common good and solidarity when they are expressed in terms of political values.'
24   Rawls, *The Law of Peoples*, pp.132–3.

The second issue is this: what are we to do with that part of a comprehensive doctrine which lies outside the consensus? Is it not possible that the most interesting, challenging, distinctive and important things that the believers in a reasonable comprehensive doctrine feel they have to offer in the public sphere may be resolutely relegated to the private and ecclesiastical spheres by Rawls and his ilk because they do not lie in the consensual overlap? Religion in general, in Rawls' scheme, is still for the most part to be confined to the private realm, and its voice is not welcome in the public sphere unless it comes to endorse the existing overlapping consensus. In the public sphere one should refrain from using religious language, or references to the distinctive resources of a particular tradition. Beyond that, Rawls now recognizes that religion is a part of civil society which may, or may not, strengthen the civic virtues and encourage attachment to democracy.

While planning to pursue this argument, and suggest that the world faiths have a duty and an opportunity to 'speak truth to power' and have relevant and important things to say in the public sphere, I was impressed by the oddity of the situation. In America, we have a very religious country, in which religion increasingly clearly shapes political thought, policy and behaviour, and yet it has an increasingly aggressively secular intellectual establishment which nurtures suspicion, misunderstanding and sometimes hostility towards religion, and often regards religion as such as primitive, divisive and dangerous. Religious arguments may be admitted by these secular gatekeepers to the public realm only if translated without remainder into secular language. The secular view is thus privileged, and the gatekeepers are self-appointed in a society that is deeply religious. Furthermore the whole debate seems strangely parochial, and isolated from what is happening in the rest of the world, let alone in the heartland of America. In a world that is so full of strongly held and powerful religious beliefs, we surely need a far broader and more hospitable forum if religious views are to be challenged and positive religious insights enabled to contribute to public debate, and enrich the life of society. What would the world today be like if Gandhi's sometimes eccentric religiopolitical views had been disallowed, and as a consequence unable to influence Martin Luther King, or Nelson Mandela, or many another? Rawls and his ilk are apparently in fundamental agreement with Fukuyama about the place of religion in the public sphere. Neither appears to have much sympathy with, or understanding of, a typical Muslim, or a right-wing evangelical Christian, for that matter.

John Howard Yoder has suggested that the real test of the value of a common moral language 'must be not the times we find ourselves agreeing with "men of good will" (especially not if they be Western humanists); it must be the capacity of this line of argument to illuminate meaningful conversations with Idi Amin or Khomeini or Chairman Mao'.[25] If there is a sense in which we share with these ogres, and with Osama bin Laden, Yasser Arafat and Ariel Sharon a common set of basic moral principles, this might form the basis for a significant discussion. The haunting suspicion persists that we are now talking of different and incompatible understandings of the right and the good, resting on radically different theologies. These differences must be confronted directly. But what a dull and petty public forum Rawls would leave us with.

Common morality, including natural law thinking, may be important, useful and even necessary – or it may be trivial or even idolatrous. But surely the task of the Church is to offer its distinctive insights and challenges rather than jumping on the bandwagon and announcing the moral truths that everyone is affirming anyway? Today's challenge is to engage directly and honestly with the often extreme theologies which actually influence the way individuals and communities construe their world and determine their behaviour. And many of these theologies and world-views are labelled 'apocalyptic'. We have to learn how to engage with what Peter Berger labels 'furious religion' as well as the forms of religion that we consider to be relatively benign.

25   John Howard Yoder (1984), *The Priestly Kingdom: Social Ethics as Gospel*, Notre Dame: University of Notre Dame Press, p.42.

Chapter 5

The Rebirth of Apocalyptic

In an hour the event of 9/11 seemed to destroy the assumed invulnerability of the world's only superpower. It shook to their foundations all sorts of assumptions about politics, culture and religion. It suggested that we were all living in an apocalyptic age and that we need a new language – or an old language revived – if we are to understand and respond appropriately and faithfully to what is happening. The conventional forms of language and of political and religious discourse in the secular West seemed inadequate to the new task, understanding and responding to this turning point in history.

'Ordinary Words were Quite Inadequate'

In similar times of crisis, in the face of earth-shattering events which challenge so many previously assured assumptions about the world, people – often quite secular people – have turned back to traditional forms of religious discourse to describe and interpret what is happening. Everyday ordinary language seems quite incapable of fulfilling this task. It is part of the argument of this book that, if we turn back to examine again the type of apocalyptic thought and language which is closest to us – particularly Biblical apocalyptic – we may be able better to understand and respond to what is happening in this age of terror, and the strange and sometimes terrible forms of discourse which are used, on both sides, to explain, to exhort and to justify.

Back in the 1940s, for instance, there was another gigantically significant turning point in history, when the first atomic bomb was tested in the New Mexico desert. This made even leading scientific protagonists in the development of the bomb at a loss for words, and often enough they fell back on classical religious forms of discourse. Robert Oppenheimer, one of the leading scientists involved in the development of the bomb, spoke of 'the strong, sustained awesome roar which warned of doomsday and made us feel that we puny things were blasphemous to dare tamper with the forces hitherto reserved to the Almighty'. Ordinary words were quite inadequate to describe what had happened and its significance. He declared at that time that scientists had now 'known sin'. Oppenheimer found that

49

he could only express his feelings as he observed the test with words from the *Bhagavad Gita*:

> If the radiance of a thousand suns
> were to burst into the sky,
> that would be like the radiance of the Mighty One.

As he watched the mushroom cloud rise ominously above the desert, another line from the *Gita* came to mind: 'I am become Death, the shatterer of worlds.'[1]

Winston Churchill, on hearing of the test, commented, 'This atomic bomb is the Second Coming in wrath.'[2] And when the first bomb was dropped in devastating anger, the tail gunner of the Enola Gay described the experience as 'a peep into hell'.[3] Henry Wieman declared that 'The bomb that fell on Hiroshima cut history in two like a knife ... That cut is more abrupt, decisive and revolutionary than the cut made by the star over Bethlehem.'[4] That last remark may well be considered an exaggeration, but it is a clear indication that the cosmic significance of the coming of the atomic bomb was clearly recognized, and there was a deep uncertainty as to how to interpret and respond to this great event.

In our day it is clear that the events of 9/11 were a vastly important turning point. We all remember what we were doing when the news of 9/11 broke – another event that 'cut history in two like a knife'. I first heard of the attacks on the World Trade Center and the Pentagon when I was boarding a bus in Edinburgh. The driver had a radio on, and told me what was happening as we spoke. My immediate reaction was that this was unreal, a fantasy generated by a diseased mind, a rerun, perhaps, of the broadcasting of H.G. Wells' *War of the Worlds* that caused panic in New York in the late 1930s. Such things do not happen in our secure and ordered world. We have become accustomed to imagining that we are invulnerable; the horrors happen far away, or on our television screens. But quickly it became clear that this time the horrifying events in New York and Washington were real.

The twin towers of the World Trade Center and the Pentagon were, of course, immensely powerful symbolic edifices, shrines of economic and military power. That was precisely why they were chosen for attack by assailants who were well aware of the language of symbolism, and saw their actions as communications which were part of a cosmic religious drama, and indeed which were justified as acts of obedience to the command of God.

---

1   Robert Junck (1960), *Brighter than a Thousand Suns*, Harmondsworth: Penguin, p.183.
2   J. Garrison (1980), *From Hiroshima to Harrisburg*, London: SCM, p.21.
3   Garrison, *From Hiroshima to Harrisburg*, p.25.
4   Garrison, *From Hiroshima to Harrisburg*, p.68.

Ramzi Yousef, the designer of the earlier attempt to bomb the World Trade Center in 1996, declared that his goal was to make America suffer casualties on the scale of the bombings of Hiroshima and Nagasaki because 'this is the way you invented ... *the only language in which someone can deal with you*'.[5] And Osama bin Laden, in his videotaped address of 7 October 2001 said:

> They have been telling the world falsehoods that they are fighting terrorism. In a nation at the far end of the world, Japan, hundreds of thousands, young and old were killed and this is not a world crime. To them it is not a clear issue. A million children in Iraq, to them this is not a clear issue ... As to America, I say to it and its people a few words: I swear to God that America will not live in peace before peace reigns in Palestine, and before all the army of infidels depart the land of Muhammad, peace be upon him.[6]

The attack on the twin towers and the Pentagon was designed not only as a communication to those who were believed to have become deaf, but, chillingly, the horror of 9/11 was enacted consciously as a kind of liturgical act, undertaken after ritual purification and a process of spiritual preparation. We have now the final instructions to the hijackers of 11 September. They consist almost entirely of what one might quite properly call a kind of 'spiritual direction'. Rather than outlining the tactics for taking over the planes and flying them into their targets, the hijackers were enjoined thus:

> Purify your soul from all unclean things. Completely forget something called 'this world' ... Bless your body with some verses of the Qur'an, the luggage, clothes, the knife, your personal effects, your ID, passport and all your papers ... Do not seem confused or show signs of nervous tension. Be happy, optimistic, calm because you are heading for a deed that God loves and will accept ... Smile in the face of hardship, young man, for you are heading toward paradise ... Remember this is a battle for the sake of God ... Either end your life while praying, seconds before the target, or make your last words: 'There is no God but God. Muhammad is his messenger.'[7]

Here we have 'furious religion' indeed. When I reached home and switched on the TV and saw the horror of what was really happening, I instinctively reached, not for any of the volumes in John Gray's bookshelf of irrelevant ideologies, but for my Bible, and I read there the account of the predicted destruction of another great building also charged with

---

5 Cited in Charles Townshend (2002), *Terrorism – A Very Short Introduction*, Oxford: OUP, p.111; emphasis mine.

6 The full text is in Bruce Lincoln (2003), *Holy Terrors: Thinking about Religion after September 11*, Chicago: University of Chicago Press, pp.102–3.

7 Bruce Lincoln (2003), *Holy Terrors: Thinking about Religion after September 11*, Chicago: University of Chicago Press, pp.93–8.

powerful symbolism. The passage was Mark 13, commonly known as 'the little Apocalypse':

> As Jesus came out of the temple, one of his disciples said to him, 'Look, Teacher, what large stones and what large buildings!' Then Jesus asked him, 'Do you see these great buildings? Not one stone will be left here upon another, all will be thrown down.' When he was sitting on the Mount of Olives opposite the temple, Peter, James, John and Andrew asked him privately, 'Tell us, when will this be, and what will be the sign that all these things are about to be accomplished?' Then Jesus began to say to them, 'Beware that no one leads you astray. Many will come in my name and say, "I am he!" and they will lead many astray. When you hear of wars and rumours of wars, do not be alarmed, this must take place, but the end is still to come. For nation will rise against nation, and kingdom against kingdom; there will be earthquakes in various places; there will be famines. This is but the beginning of the birth pangs …
>
> As for yourselves, beware; for they will hand you over to councils; and you will be beaten in synagogues; and you will stand before governors and kings because of me, as a testimony to them. And the good news must first be proclaimed to all nations … Beware, keep alert, for you do not know when the time will come.[8]

I read this and other apocalyptic passages from the Bible with a kind of fascination, and a degree of puzzlement. They come from the heart of the New Testament, and were clearly believed to be a way of communicating gospel – good news. But they did not speak of the day-to-day world I inhabit, and much of this apocalyptic scenario in the Bible I found, and still find, inaccessible. Yet this is the specific form of religious language and symbolism which is used by many who are labelled 'terrorists', and also by neoconservative Christians who are in positions of great influence in the United States today.[9] But it has been embraced down the ages particularly by humble, generous and hopeful believers as giving them guidance to living lives of faith in hard and terrifying times. Understanding and engaging with this apocalyptic language and imagery is clearly a pressing task for those who want to discern 'the signs of the times' and respond appropriately.

This little passage of Christian apocalyptic makes some points very clearly. The permanence, solidity, finality of the temple as the sign of the religious and political order is denied. It will not last; we should not put our trust in such passing symbolic structures, or in what they signify. Faithfulness will be very hard, for false messiahs and false ideas will crowd around. The temptation to recognize the pretensions of the powerful, and live in peace in a world that is dominated by lies will be compelling.

---

8   Mark 13.1–10, 33. Cf. Matthew 24.1–36; Luke 21.5–36.

9   See especially M.S. Northcott (2004), *An Angel Directs the Storm: Apocalyptic Religion and American Empire*, London: I.B. Tauris.

Violence and wars will abound, along with vast natural catastrophes. These are not signs of the impotence or the absence of God, but they are the context in which God is working out his project for good. They are, paradoxically, signs of hope, the beginning of the *birth pangs* of the new order which God will establish.

In the midst of all this turmoil there are the faithful ones. They will be persecuted and despised, but they are called to witness boldly to God's truth (the Good News) before their oppressors. They are called to be faithful, to keep alert for the fulfilment of God's promises. Somehow, strangely, in the midst of all this devastation and rage, the Good News is to be proclaimed to all nations. The saints keep alert to discern in the midst of all these horrors the fulfilment of God's purposes. They watch and they witness. They do not fight, or seek to destroy their persecutors. They wait in faith and hope, with great courage.

The most obvious and total contrast between the little apocalypse of Mark and most of the apocalyptic discourse surrounding 9/11 to which I have referred is this: in Mark the disciples, the faithful ones, are not called to kill or to fight in these wars; indeed they are called if necessary to flee, or to suffer, to endure, to attend and, above all, to wait for God to work out his purposes of good. In this little passage and its parallels we see already some of the characteristics of apocalyptic in general, and also some of the distinctive features of Christian apocalyptic. Disciples are to wait in hope and love. They are not to attempt to take things into their own hands. Above all, they are not to turn to violence. This is for disciples a time of testing, and many will fail that test and stray from the ways of truth.

Passages like the one from Mark seemed that day and since both to be challenging to me as one who tries to be a disciple, and to take the Bible seriously, and also to provide some kind of clues to the thought world that the hijackers, and bin Laden, and millions of American born-again Evangelicals, and many other religious believers today, as in the past, inhabit, and how they express their fury, their despair and their hope. My puzzlement and horror was surely part of the more general problem for us of understanding and relating to forms and expressions of religion that we see as bizarre and dangerous, and often deeply offensive: suicide bombers and hijackers, and Sharon's 'dividing wall of hostility' in the Holy Land, the present disorderly strife in occupied Iraq, and Israeli onslaughts on the West Bank.

There was thus a great deal of unabashedly and irreducibly apocalyptic religious language used about the events of 11 September, on both sides. We saw the rebirth of apocalyptic images, for good and for ill. Both sides embraced a Manichaean polarization between the absolute good – us – and the absolute evil – our antagonists. The hijackers, as we have seen, received a kind of perverse spiritual discipline as they prepared for what they understood as martyrdom, a way of witnessing with one's life to the truth. Bin Laden's broadcasts and statements reflected a characteristically apocalyptic dualism, and an extraordinary confidence that supernatural agency would ensure the rapid destruction of America.

On the other side we heard the language of a war against absolute evil, a crusade, and 'May God continue to bless America' was constantly on the lips of President Bush and many another. 'The prayer that I would like America to ask for,' he said, 'is to pray for God's protection for our land and for our people … [To pray] that there's a shield of protection, so that if the evil ones try to hit us again we've done everything we can, physically, and that there is a spiritual shield that defends this country.'[10] Indeed it has been argued that America has 'always been under the influence of an apocalyptic impulse'.[11] The war on terror is 'civilization's fight', declared President Bush. Neutrality is not possible because 'God is not neutral'.[12]

And then, here and there, quietly for the most part, there was also the deeply moving language of love, spoken through mobile phones by people about to die. But perhaps this language in the long run is at least as important as the more strident tones that dominate the world. Rowan Williams points to the contrast between the two kinds of language:

> The religious words are, in the cold light of day, the words that murderers are saying to themselves to make a martyr's drama out of a crime, the non-religious words are testimony to what religious language is supposed to be about – the triumph of pointless, gratuitous love, the affirming of faithfulness even when there is nothing to be done or salvaged.[13]

'The triumph of pointless, gratuitous love [and] the affirming of faithfulness even when there is nothing to be done or salvaged' – that, too, is apocalyptic discourse.

Apocalyptic Literature

The word 'apocalyptic' in Greek means revelation or unveiling. Hence the

---

10 Cited in Bruce Lincoln (2003), *Holy Terrors: Thinking about Religion after September 11*, Chicago: University of Chicago Press, p.46.
11 See Ira Chernus (2004), 'George W. Bush's War on Terrorism and Sin', in *Political Theology*, **5** (4), pp.411–30; M.S. Northcott (2004), *An Angel Directs the Storm: Apocalyptic Religion and American Empire*, London: I.B. Tauris; and 'Bringing on the Apocalypse', *Third Way*, Nov. 2004, pp.22–24.
12 Chernus (2004), 'George W. Bush's War', p.420.
13 Rowan Williams (2002), *Writing in the Dust: Reflections on 11th September and its Aftermath*, London: Hodder and Stoughton, pp.1–2.

last book of the New Testament, which is a classic and sustained example of apocalyptic literature, is known as Revelation, or as the Apocalypse. There are also many other examples of apocalyptic literature in the Bible (such as the 'little apocalypse' in Mark 13, and its parallels, or the Book of Daniel in the Old Testament). And, beyond the canon, there are numerous instances of apocalyptic themes in the religious literature of early Christianity and of Judaism, and rather later in Muslim literature. Furthermore there has been an extraordinary and almost continuous and sustained engagement with apocalyptic literature in Christianity, which has had a major revival in our times, both at the scholarly and at more popular circles.[14]

The 'unveiling' or revelation, in apocalyptic literature usually refers to a discernment of what is really happening, now, in the world, and its significance. Earthly tumults and wars are characteristically presented as reflections on earth of what is happening, 'for real', as it were, in the heavenly places. This revelation or unveiling is commonly associated with despair about the condition of the world, and the expectation of its imminent destruction. The earthly powers and their claims of permanence and finality are consistently challenged. Apocalyptic literature is concerned with interpreting the present situation and the power structures of today; it is not solely concerned with the future, although it characteristically presents the future, God's future, as breaking into the present. It challenges and relativizes the claims of the Powers, and accordingly gives solace and encouragement to the faithful.[15] And it is not hard to see why there is frequently a revival of apocalyptic in times of crisis, when the old landmarks seem to be eroded, and new interpretative tools are required.

Understanding Apocalyptic

Ancient systems of interpretation and 'discerning the signs of the times' carry with them risks of which we should be aware, when they are used today. The straining for the recovery of old keys for the interpretation of what is radically new and threatening has its dangers, of course. A turning to religious language and religious symbols may indicate a recognition that the issues are grave, and that unusual resources are needed to cope with

---

14 John J. Collins (1998), *The Apocalyptic Imagination: An Introduction to Jewish Apocalyptic Literature*, 2nd edn, Grand Rapids: Eerdmans; also Duane F. Watson (ed.) (2002), *The Intertexture of Apocalyptic Discourse in the New Testament*, Atlanta: SBL; Judith Kovacs and Christopher Rowland (2004), *Revelation*, Oxford: Blackwell.
15 Christopher Rowland (1982), *The Open Heaven: A Study of Apocalyptic in Judaism and Early Christianity*, London: SPCK, pp.1–2.

them, but it does not in itself guarantee that these matters will be handled wisely. Religious symbols may inflame rather than illumine, and religious rhetoric excite rather than clarify. Such religious rhetoric may be a powerful agency for recruitment, especially among those in the West who have 'grown weary of their non-religious upbringing', so that they feel no sense of purpose, and believe that they are not being allowed to contribute to some great cause.[16] Osama bin Laden, as we have seen, constantly uses the rhetoric of apocalyptic to justify his outrages and he places them in a particular apocalyptic frame.

This is precisely the point at which a major intellectual responsibility comes into view: theologians in particular are, or ought to be, people trained in the disciplined and critical investigation of religious symbolic structures, and the careful and responsible use of religious language. But we have our problems, too, the most relevant of which is how we can analyse and describe religious symbolic structures from the outside, as it were. Modern liberal intellectuals and believers are more or less excluded from the realm of apocalyptic. We find it hard to understand why and how people inhabit such structures, and allow them to shape their faith and life, for good or ill. And we presume, perhaps too quickly, that apocalyptic is primitive and perhaps inherently evil.

Yet we live in a world in which secular liberal rationalists are a small minority, and huge numbers of people understand their world in the light of religious symbolic structures that sometimes seem bizarre to others. They find in apocalyptic religion their public and political motivation and solace. There is a pressing task to understand why a young Muslim should kill himself and cause the death of thousands of innocent people, after receiving 'spiritual guidance' about his deportment in the last minutes before the disaster, his last words as recorded on the black box being 'Allah Akbar'. It can all be dismissed as pathological fanaticism, or the manipulation of religion and religious people for sordid political ends, but the task of understanding is the precondition for intelligent and effective response. And so far the efforts at understanding have not been particularly impressive or illuminating.

An immediate danger is that the events of 11 September 2001 and their aftermath will simply confirm the common western secular assumption that religion, and especially 'fundamentalist' or apocalyptic religion, is pathological, divisive, dangerous and irrational. There is a long and sad history showing how western secular failure to understand particularly radical Islam has led to ill-advised and sometimes disastrous action in many

---

16 Suleyman tells me he grew weary of his non-religious upbringing: 'I felt like I had no sense of purpose. I felt as if I wasn't being allowed to contribute to anything' (Burhan Wazir, 'The Talibanisation of Britain proceeds', *New Statesman*, 11 February 2002, p.33).

contexts. This illustrates a more general problem, that the West 'has for so long relegated religion to the realm of the personal and the domestic that it left many of us insensitive to the extent to which religion and politics intertwine in much of the rest of the world. Such an insensitivity can and does lead ... to uninformed and potentially costly foreign policy choices, as in reactions to the Iranian revolution'.[17] Gary Sick, for instance, who was the principal White House aide for Iran on the National Security Council in the 1980s, deplored the failure of the US policymakers to appreciate the significance of radical and apocalyptic religion in the third world. 'There are,' he wrote, 'contradictions between Khomeini's Islamic, theocratic revolution and the Western tradition of secularizing revolutions. In my view, this tension between the secular and the religious was a major contributing factor to the failure of both Iranians and Westerners to recognise the revolution in its early stages and to gauge properly its actual course and eventual outcome. We are all prisoners of our own cultural assumptions, more than we care to admit ... The participation of the church in a revolutionary movement was neither new nor particularly disturbing, but the notion of a popular revolution leading to the establishment of a theocratic state seemed so unlikely as to be absurd.'[18]

This difficulty of understanding was underlined in the 1980s by the role of Terry Waite in the Levant as the emissary of the Archbishop of Canterbury. Before his own kidnapping it seemed that Terry Waite was better able than the formal diplomats to understand the radical Islamic forces and negotiate with them, precisely because he was himself a religious man, and the representative of a major religious leader. Terry Waite was able to speak with terrorists at a serious level, and rejected the Thatcherite assumption that to refuse to talk with terrorists and deny them a voice in the media was to deprive them of 'the oxygen of publicity'.[19] Other hostages at the time, such as John McCarthy and Brian Keenan, show that the difficulty of understanding went both ways. Although neither of them claimed to be an observant Christian, their captors automatically provided them with Bibles, assuming that they would read and meditate on their holy book each day. The possibility of atheism or agnosticism was not conceivable to their captors.[20]

---

17 Douglas Johnston and Cynthia Sampson (eds) (1994), *Religion – The Missing Dimension of Statecraft*, Oxford: OUP, p.xv.

18 Gary Sick (1985), *All Fall Down: America's Tragic Encounter with Iran*, New York: Penguin, pp.192–3.

19 On the issue of 'talking with terrorists', see the discussion in Lee Griffith (2002), *The War on Terrorism and the Terror of God*, Grand Rapids: Eerdmans, pp.220–21.

20 See Terry Waite (1993), *Taken on Trust*, London: Hodder and Stoughton; Brian Keenan (1992), *An Evil Cradling*, London: Hutchison; John McCarthy (2001), 'Introduction' to Matthew Sturgis, *It Ain't Necessarily So*, London: Headline.

Exploration of apocalyptic in foundational holy writings, in movements down the centuries, and in today's world, may shed some light on what is happening today, and perhaps even on how most appropriately to respond. Examining an apocalyptic scenario may help a little to explain why people blow themselves up on the streets of Israel, fly planes to create a destructive inferno in the twin towers, and proclaim, despite all appearances, the imminent end of the world's only superpower, the United States of America. And some American actions and policies are best explained by the influence of a certain kind of apocalyptic thought on the inner circles around President Bush. Engaging critically with the role of apocalyptic in our own tradition, in our theology and in today's expressions of faith may also serve both to deepen understanding and to give us resources for channeling apocalyptic thought into constructive and illuminating directions.

And perhaps a question for us is not so much why people fall victim to, or embrace, a pathological apocalypticism, but rather why many people in the West who are themselves believers have difficulty in understanding or appreciating or engaging with an apocalyptic faith.

Christian Apocalyptic

Listen to a leading modern scholar who gives an account of the major features of apocalyptic literature, especially as represented by the New Testament Book of Revelation, which expresses, he says, alternative conceptions of the world, its history and its future through

> a concern with the contradiction between God's rule over creation and the apparently unchecked dominance of evil in the world, the hope of an impending final resolution of history in which God will bring eternal good out of all the evils of this world and renew his creation ... it draws [us] into different ways of seeing things ... It speaks to a world whose imaginative view of the world is controlled by the power and propaganda of the dominant political and economic system. By envisioning the same world from the perspective of God's kingdom ... *Revelation liberates its readers from the dominant world-view. It exposes the idolatry which from top to bottom infuses and inspires the political, economic and social realities in which its readers live, and calls them to an uncompromising Christian witness to the true God who despite earthly appearances is sovereign. By seeing the world differently, readers are enabled to live and to die differently* ... They are empowered ... to live in hope of the coming of God's kingdom as the ultimate truth of the world which must prevail over all that presently opposes God's rule.[21]

---

21 Richard Bauckham (2001), 'Revelation', in John Barton and John Muddiman (eds), *The Oxford Bible Commentary*, Oxford: Oxford University Press, pp.1287–8; my italics.

Apocalyptic, as it were, comes to life, or is reborn, in times of crisis.[22] Characteristically, but not invariably, it arises among groups that despair about the conditions of the present world order, and believe in its imminent destruction or overthrow.[23] Apocalyptic has, I suggest, some functions which are particularly relevant to our present discussion. In the first place, apocalyptic claims to reveal, unveil, make manifest the inner reality of what is actually happening in the world today. It is concerned to understand things as they are now, not simply to predict the future.[24] It seeks to discern what is happening in history, and what God is calling his people to do. The powers of evil and the forces that have presented themselves as angels of light are unmasked, and believers are enabled to discern what is really happening. Apocalyptic denies the finality and acceptability of the existing order of things (*pace* Francis Fukuyama). The pretensions of rulers and dominant authorities are cut down to size and relativized. Apocalyptic declares that the existing powers that be are not the final manifestation of God's purposes; their days are numbered. An alternative order, in which the faithful, the weak and the excluded will have an honoured place, is not only possible, but it is promised, and it will break in and disrupt the existing order. Apocalyptic thus nourishes a confident hope not only that things *can* be different, but that they *will* be different, for, if believers are faithful, God will bring out of the present disorder a new era which will be characterized by peace and justice and the vindication of the oppressed.

In much, perhaps most, apocalyptic, as in the book of Revelation, alongside a radical political critique, there is much imagery of a holy war. In this war, the weak, despite appearances and expectations, are the real victors. The holy war may be a spiritual or a real conflict; God may take the initiative, or call on the saints to wage war on his behalf. And 'waging war' (or Jihad, for that matter) may simply be a metaphor for keeping the faith in times of persecution – or it may be real and savage war, waged without restraint. But the Christian nature of authentically Christian apocalyptic is represented by the centrality in the Book of Revelation of Jesus, the triumphant Lamb that has been slain and who is praised by the faithful, singing a new song.[25] He has already won the last battle, absorbing in his own flesh and in his dying the wrath and violence of the forces of evil in the world.

There are, of course, specific problems associated with a lively apocalyptic world-view. In the first place, the dualism of Jerusalem and Babylon in the

22 H.H. Rowley (1947), *The Relevance of Apocalyptic*, London: Lutterworth, p.8.

23 Rowland (1982), *Open Heaven*, pp.1–2.

24 Christopher Rowland (1982), *Open Heaven*, p.2.

25 See John Howard Yoder (1988), 'To Serve our God and to Rule the World', *The Annual of the Society of Christian Ethics*, pp.3–14.

Book of Revelation (or their equivalents in other systems of apocalyptic thought) presents as central to its radical political critique a polarization between absolute evil and absolute good, which is at the least a colossal simplification of any actual situation in the world. It can breed a very dangerous and unqualified self-righteousness. And these distortions can have a malign effect on political judgments and political action, as can a relativism which hesitates to make any clear distinction between good and evil. In politics, many a time the leader has to choose the lesser evil, and efforts to create the perfect society or to destroy 'the evil Empire' lead to disaster. But apocalyptic, for the most part, is not written for the rulers who wrestle with the ambiguities of politics, but rather for the powerless and oppressed, to give them hope. But time and again in history, as still today, rulers and the powerful have used apocalyptic imagery and language to justify and explain their purposes.

A second major problem is that, while much apocalyptic encourages the saints to be patient until God brings their deliverance, other forms encourage the faithful to take things into their own hands, so that they understand themselves as saints combating and destroying unqualified evil in the name of God and at the direct command of God. This is not something that I find in the book of Revelation or as a significant element in Jewish and Christian apocalyptic generally, but it is certainly prominent in varieties of apocalyptic which are influential in today's world. In all forms of apocalyptic there tends to be a stress on the imagery of the holy war, often a spiritual rather than an actual war. Those who perish in that war are regarded as virtuous martyrs and saints. John, the writer of Revelation, radically transforms the expectation of a coming war in which God's people are to fight and vanquish their enemies. For him the faithful are to *wait*, holding fast to truth, and being willing to suffer, while the decisive action has already been undertaken by Christ, the Lamb.[26]

More positively, apocalyptic holds out an open future and offers hope to the poor, the powerless and the excluded. Its message to the powerful, the prosperous and the complacent is a word of judgment, and a challenge to hear the uncomfortable word that the Spirit is saying to the churches and to the world. And, for us, this demands careful attention to questions such as why young men will blow themselves to death and destroy multitudes of innocent lives in the process, believing that this is the will of God, and that their act is heroic. I will return to these issues in the next two chapters.

Apocalyptic language is commonly, but certainly not always, the discourse of people who feel themselves weak, marginalized, oppressed and

---

26 Richard Bauckham (1993a), *The Climax of Prophecy: Studies in the Book of Revelation*, Edinburgh: T. & T. Clark, p.xv.

forgotten.[27] It is a language of hope for change, and it is a language of judgment. It is language that motivates powerfully, for good or ill, and it is language which polarizes between Jerusalem and Babylon, the good and the evil, the saints and the wicked in a quite Manichaean way. This kind of polarization is always, of course, a huge simplification at the very least. In the real world we have much of the time to deal in subtle shades of grey rather than a contrast between black and white. But sometimes we need to highlight the awfulness of evil or the mystery of goodness. In Rowan Williams' words:

> The mythology of the IRA and of al-Qaida alike promises to give your life and death the most immense significance – heroism, martyrdom – you take control of your destiny by pledging it to a cause that is beyond moral question, even beyond the possibility of ultimate failure. You will not die meaninglessly; that is reserved for your victims.[28]

Apocalyptic is a major way of sustaining meaning and hope, the kind of hope that keeps people going when all around seems hopeless. In the South African theologian Denise Ackermann's words, hope 'acts like a powerful alchemy enabling human beings to emerge from ghastly circumstances with their humanity intact ... Hope is resistance. It actively resists the void of hopelessness'.[29]

The Triumphant Lamb

The central thing about Christian apocalyptic, as I read the Book of Revelation, is this: at the heart of all the struggles, all the sufferings, all the anger and rage is not so much the victory of the saints in a bloody battle as the worship by the 144 000, who are the first-fruits of God's great harvest. They now sing a new song in honour of the Lamb who has been slain and has absorbed into himself and overcome the rage and fear and violence of the world. The writer of the sustained apocalypse that is the Book of Revelation transforms the tradition he inherited, which looked to a messianic war in which God's people fight with ruthless courage to win a great and definitive victory over their enemies. Instead John depicts the saints as being called to faithful and courageous participation in God's spiritual war against evil, following up the decisive victory that

---

27 On this see the sociological literature on millenarianism, such as Norman Cohn (1970), *The Pursuit of the Millennium*, London: Paladin.
28 R. Williams (2002), *Writing in the Dust*, p.41.
29 Denise Ackermann (1992), 'The Alchemy of Hope', in Dennis Brutus (ed.), *A Book of Hope*, Claremont, RSA: David Philip, pp.28–9.

Jesus has achieved on the cross.[30] Their task is more to worship than to fight.

The image of the Lamb evokes Passover memories: it is God who delivers his people; they do not do it by their own efforts, rage and force of arms. It also evokes and interprets the event of cross and resurrection, for then and there, in an event in time, the determinative victory has been won. The saints leave vengeance to God; their task is to demonstrate the power of the powerless, 'strength made perfect in weakness'.[31] The primary task of the saints is to celebrate and declare the victory of the Lamb, who died for others, and who rules in heaven and is destined to rule fully on earth. The saints do not withdraw from economic and political involvement. They are not passive but publicly challenging. They are called to expose and denounce the idolatry of Babylon, the arrogance of power and wealth.

And they look forward to the coming as a gift of a new heaven and a new earth, given by the One who sits on the throne and proclaims, 'Behold I make all things new!' 'He will wipe every tear from their eyes. There shall be an end to death and to mourning and crying and pain, for the old order has passed away!'[32] The false and evil ones will be condemned to 'the second death'. But the city of God is not a refuge for the saints from the sinful world. It is of cosmic and universal significance:

> By its light shall the nations walk, and to it the kings of the earth shall bring their splendour. The gates of the city shall never be shut by day, nor will there be any night there. The splendour and wealth of the nations shall be brought into it, but nothing unclean shall enter, nor anyone whose ways are foul or false.[33]

In the middle of the city flows 'the river of the water of life', with a 'tree of life' on either side. And 'the leaves of the trees are for the healing of the nations'.[34]

The existence of the fellowship of the faithful ones and the way they organize their common life is a sign of the reign of the Lamb and a foretaste of the Kingdom of heaven. This is a community which witnesses to the importance of non-violence and peace, and demonstrates 'a new way of living and dying'.[35] It waits in humble confidence, willing if necessary to suffer with its Lord and with neighbours near and far. It nurtures among

---

30   Richard Bauckham (1993), *The Climax of Prophecy: Studies in the Book of Revelation*, Edinburgh: T. & T. Clark, p.xv.
31   II Corinthians 12.9.
32   Revelation 21.4.
33   Revelation 21.24–7.
34   Revelation 22.2.
35   Bauckham, *Climax of Prophecy*, p.xv.

its members a new understanding of virtue, but that is the subject of the next two chapters. And all this is of continuing political relevance today in the aftermath of 9/11 through the witness of Martin Luther King, Mahatma Gandhi, Nelson Mandela and Desmond Tutu, and many others who eschew vengeance and pursue peace and truth and seek justice, forgiveness and reconciliation with a hopeful confidence and joy.

I can think of no better way to conclude this chapter than with a poem by Godfrey Rust that explores the role of the Lamb and his disciples in today's apocalyptic world:

> Who is our enemy
> and what can we fight him with?
> Where are our allies? Where was God
> on September the Eleventh? He was begging
> in old clothes in the subway
> beneath the World Trade Center.
> He was homeless in Gaza,
> imprisoned in Afghanistan,
> starving in Somalia,
> dying of Aids in an Angolan slum,
> suffering everywhere in this fast-shrinking world:
> and boarding a plane unwittingly in Boston,
> heading for a meeting on the 110th floor.
> When the time came he stretched his arms out once again
> to take the dreadful impact that would pierce his side.
> His last message on his fading cell phone
> once more to ask forgiveness for them all, before
> his body fell under the weight of so much evil.
> We bring our cameras to his massive tomb
> for any chance of resurrection, now we know
> the kind of story that it really is,
> united by this common enemy,
> sin's terrorism – that we never dreamed
> could bring such devastation. This is war:
> We line our weapons up: faith, hope obedience,
> prayer, forgiveness, justice;
> the explosive power of love.[36]

---

36 From 'September 11, 2001' © Godfrey Rust. The complete poem may be found at www.wordsout.co.uk. Used here by kind permission.

We now turn to discuss some of the ways in which an apocalyptic expression of the Christian gospel, which takes sin and evil, and forgiveness, with profound seriousness has been worked out down the ages, and may be constructive and challenging in the public sphere today.

Chapter 6

Conflicting Virtues: Saints or Heroes?

Why is a discussion of virtues and vices and the conflicts between them important in a book that is primarily concerned with trying to understand and respond to the present world situation, in a time of terror, particularly in its religious and political dimensions? Part of the answer should be that there is already a vigorous debate about virtues and vices taking place, with the American neoconservative thinker, Robert D. Kaplan, writing a book, *Warrior Politics: Why Leadership Demands a Pagan Ethos*,[1] in which he argues that the traditional Judaeo-Christian understanding and practice of virtue is enervating in the public sphere, and makes effective political leadership and military action in times of crisis impossible. Hence, in the present situation, he argues that we should return to the old heroic pagan virtues of the ancient world, and their modern presentation by such as Machiavelli, if we are to hope to achieve anything effective in a time of terror.

Why are the virtues – and the vices – still important? One may answer this question in terms of contemporary academic debates. But it is also true that a great deal of collective and individual behaviour today is shaped by understandings of what virtue is, understandings that are often wildly at variance with one another. One person's virtue is another person's vice. The activities of suicide bombers, or of soldiers engaged in what they understand as 'humanitarian intervention', are regarded by some as vicious and by the main agents themselves as virtuous. Ideas of virtue and of vice are incorporated into patterns of behaviour which they shape but which are often profoundly controversial. The next chapter will discuss some of these patterns as they are expressed in today's world. The present chapter will examine some of the basic continuing tensions in the understanding (and the practice) of virtue.

Most modern moral philosophy and discussion of ethics centres on specific concrete decisions, and suggests guidelines such as duty, or the pursuit of the greatest good of the greatest number, as providing guidance for determining what actions are good. We need, however, to be concerned with more than concrete moral decisions, and we should recognize that the choice before us is frequently not a matter of choosing quite simply between

---

1 Robert D. Kaplan (2003), *Warrior Politics: Why Leadership Demands a Pagan Ethos*, New York: Vintage Books.

a good and an evil course of action. In a fallen world it is often necessary to discern and choose the lesser evil, and pursue a course of action which is not in itself good, and may indeed be sinful. Virtue ethics, however, affirms that a good *person* is one who is highly likely to do good actions without calculation or hesitation; for her doing good is a natural expression of who she is, a virtuous person who unconsciously is inclined to do the good.

And there are praiseworthy actions of a sort which cannot be understood as duties or as demanded by some kind of moral calculus, but are indubitably virtuous. They go beyond the requirements of duty, or of 'ordinary' morality. For example, a soldier who throws himself over an unexploded grenade in order, through his dying, to save the lives of his comrades may well be called a hero or even a saint, but his action is not responding to a categorical imperative binding on everyone, and if it were the result of a Kantian 'universalizing one's maxim' then all the soldiers should throw themselves on the grenade and all would die. The soldier's giving up of his life for the sake of his comrades is not the result of an elaborate calculus of the probable consequences of his act. It is a virtuous act of the sort that comes naturally to a virtuous person because virtue has been imbibed from her upbringing and personal convictions.[2] Thus the truly virtuous person, the Saint or the Hero, goes far beyond the conventional and universally binding canons of 'everyday morality'.

Virtues are important; every culture and society recognizes virtues and vices, and presents virtues as commended and praised models of behaviour. Characteristically an understanding of virtue is shaped by religion, but any society, social institution or army depends on having some commonly accepted standards of virtue and of vice which are constantly inculcated reviewed and debated. The basic stories of a culture or society – what Alasdair MacIntyre calls its 'canon' – among other things explore issues of virtue and vice, and present models for emulation or rejection. These stories – the Bible, Homer and the Qu'ran are relevant examples – are not simply retold to children at their mother's knee; they are explored, and reflected upon in sagas and epics, in drama (particularly effectively in Greek tragedy), in poetry and constantly in philosophy and theology. But above all, perhaps, models of virtue and of vice are tried out in the practices of life, in the choices we make, in the ways we understand ourselves as moral agents.

Alastair MacIntyre famously deplored the 'startling number of differences and incompatibilities' in the various accounts of virtue which have arisen within the western tradition in modern times and which are still influential. What we have today, he declared, is a set of totally incompatible

---

2 See J.O. Urmson (1958), 'Saints and Heroes', in A.I. Melden (ed.), *Essays in Moral Philosophy*, Seattle: University of Washington Press, pp.198–216.

understandings of virtue, and 'different theories about what a virtue is'.[3] MacIntyre discerned fundamental differences between the Homeric and the philosophic accounts, and in particular he saw the New Testament's presentation of the virtues as in basic tension with both. Such fundamental moral incompatibilities about the virtues were for MacIntyre central to his despairing attitude towards what he saw as the moral and ideological fragmentation and disintegration of western culture. But perhaps he underestimated the extent to which there has always been, in every culture and society, and between cultures and societies, significant disagreement about the virtues, about what actions are virtuous, and about the characteristics of the virtuous person. Certainly it is right to say that 'Accounts of the moral life in terms of virtue seem destined to vie with one another in the contemporary political arena.'[4]

Since *After Virtue* was written in the early 1980s we have become vividly aware that the problem is a global one which cannot be confined to western culture, or attributed solely to the legacy of the Enlightenment. The world is fuller than we once thought of conflicting and mutually unintelligible understandings of the virtues, which sometimes are death-dealing and bitter. The Enlightenment hope of producing a universal, rational and godless image of virtue has failed. Religion in a variety of forms is still robustly active in shaping a diversity of understandings of virtue. And MacIntyre's rather gloomy suggestion at the conclusion of *After Virtue* that the virtues and serious moral enquiry might in the new Dark Ages in which we live be preserved in small communities of faith may be more relevant now than when MacIntyre first wrote. I would suggest the early Church, and one hopes also today's churches, can be seen as networks of just such morally serious communities of faith engaging in depth with the nature of virtue in the light of the gospel.

When we speak of ethical fragmentation we are not dealing with a unique expression of modernity or post-modernity. Today's situation has its parallels in the past. And in many ways the past is very much alive today. So we look back before we look forward in the hope that the past may yield some helpful insights for today.

Classical Models of Public Virtue

In the classical world the virtues of the warrior hero were far more

---

3   Alastair MacIntyre (1981), *After Virtue: A Study in Moral Theory*, London: Duckworth, p.171.

4   Charles Pinches (2000), 'Virtue', in Adrian Hastings (ed.), *The Oxford Companion to Christian Thought*, Oxford: Clarendon Press.

prominent than those of the saint, although it is certainly true to say that a philosopher such as Socrates adopted a lifestyle which had many 'saintly' qualities. The Goddess Virtus or Arete was seen as the personification of the manly public virtues. The iconography presented her as bearing a sword in her right hand and a spear in her left. On her head was a helmet, and under her right foot there lay the helmet of a defeated adversary. This icon clearly affirmed the centrality of military and aggressive excellence in the popular and officially sponsored understanding of virtue in the Graeco-Roman world. The image of the virtuous warrior hero was rooted in the Homeric epics, and was solidly military. And it still lives powerfully on, as in Hobbes, who wrote, 'Force and fraud are in war the two cardinal virtues.'[5] Yet the virtue of the warrior hero has been shaped and reshaped constantly throughout history, and is still a lively issue, as we shall see in the next chapter.

The classical account of virtue found a rather different, and somewhat less military, shape in the philosophers' explorations of the nature of virtue. Socrates taught that virtue was a science: you learned through trial and error and through reflection what virtue is, and how it applies to one. But the key issue for him and for most of the Greek philosophers was not so much to know what the virtues are, but rather how to be virtuous.[6] This knowledge of how to be virtuous was in part knowledge of oneself, and in part knowledge of the goal or end of human life. Such knowledge, when put into practice, ensures that our actions are virtuous. In relation to discussions of virtue, as in all his life, Socrates was a 'gadfly', questioning established certainties and opening up new possibilities, as when he said: 'I tell you that virtue is not given by money, but that from virtue come money and every other good of man, public as well as private.'[7]

Plato expounded what later became known as the 'cardinal virtues' of temperance, courage, prudence and justice. Aristotle saw a virtue as the mean between two extremes, and identified the major public virtues as courage, temperance, liberality, magnificence ('the spending of large sums tastefully'), good temper, and – note this clearly – *pride*. Pride was for the one who was known in the Middle Ages as '*the* philosopher' the crown of the virtues. As MacIntyre points out, 'The only place in Aristotle's account of the virtues where anything resembling humility is mentioned, it is as a vice, and patience is not mentioned at all by Aristotle.'[8] And in this he reflected the common assumption of most ancient societies, and the persistent belief that a major model of virtue was the proud warrior hero.

---

5   *Leviathan*, 1.13.
6   W.K.C. Guthrie (1971), *Socrates*, Cambridge: Cambridge University Press, pp.130–39.
7   Plato, *Apology*, 30.b.
8   Alastair MacIntyre (1981), *After Virtue*, p.165.

Pride, or *megalopsuchia*, perhaps equally well translated as self-confidence, high-mindedness and self-respect, held the pre-eminent place in Aristotle's ethical thought.[9] The one who exemplifies this central virtue is not only proud, but rather unconcerned for others and lacking in modesty. In many ways he appears to be an arrogant and self-confident aristocratic warrior. Poor people, according to this tradition, could not be expected to be virtuous in the true sense. All that was open to them, in terms of virtue, was obedience, conscientious fulfilment of their lowly tasks, and a proper humility, recognizing and accepting their lowly status. The ordinary workman, mechanic or servant was a *Banausos*, defined in Liddell and Scott's *Greek–English Lexicon* as 'a mechanic' belonging to 'a class that leads a sedentary life, despised among warlike or nomad people, base, ignoble', whereas *Banausia* is 'the practice of a mere mechanical art. The life and habits of a mere mechanic, hence, vulgarity, bad taste'. When this view of virtue and who could be virtuous was translated into Latin it is not surprising that *megalopsuche* was translated as *superbia* or superiority, being above or superior to others. According to Liddell and Scott's *A Latin Dictionary*, *superbia* means 'loftiness, haughtiness, pride, conceit, vanity. And the Greek terms related to *tapeinos* (or humility) were translated as *humilis* and its cognates, meaning, according to Liddell and Scott, 'low, lowly, base, mean, humble, obscure, insignificant'.

The Christian Virtue of Humility

For the early Christian Church these classical accounts of virtue posed a serious difficulty, not just because of their embeddedness in classical pagan culture. This unease was partly because these pagan listings of virtues were aristocratic; they seemed to apply mainly or entirely to the prosperous and powerful, rather than the poor, the oppressed and the weak – precisely the people who formed the backbone of the earliest Christian congregations. It was not enough simply to add to the classical listings of the virtues what became know as the 'theological virtues' of faith, hope and love, or charity. These did not sit easily, in their priorities and emphases, with the classical listings, and while one could reinterpret some of the pagan virtues in the light of these new Christian virtues, they were not of the same order, and there was a deep underlying conflict. Aristotle, for instance, regarded humility as a vice. While one could to some extent reconceptualize justice

---

9   Sir David Ross (1954), *The Nichomathean Ethics of Aristotle*, Oxford: Oxford University Press; IV.3 is concerned with pride. Edward Moore has a useful discussion of the meaning of *megalopsuchia* in his *An Introduction to Aristotle's Ethics*, 2nd edn, Oxford: Rivingtons, 1878, pp.233–9.

in the light of charity or love, there was for Christians a huge problem both in embracing a set of virtues so military, and especially in treating pride, or 'magnificence', as a virtue at all. Indeed the early Church regarded pride and the 'military virtues' except for courage emphatically as vices.

For the early Christians pride was the central vice, humility in a way the all-encompassing virtue. What was at issue was not only humility towards God, but also, and derivatively, humility in our relationship to people of all sorts. After all, Christians regarded the Messiah, Jesus, as one who set aside his divine status and humbled himself in order to become human, and die as the Suffering Servant. The Letter to the Philippians celebrates the humility of Jesus in the incarnation:

> He was in the form of God; yet he laid no claim to equality with God, but made himself nothing, assuming the form of a slave. Bearing the human likeness, sharing the human lot, he humbled himself, and was obedient, even to the point of death, death on a cross![10]

Notice that this interpretation of the incarnation emphasizes the chosen humiliation of the Son of God, and his identification not only with the human lot in general, but particularly with the slaves, the lowest of the low, who were forced to exemplify what now became another new Christian virtue, obedience, above all to the Christ who humbled himself. This choosing of the virtue of humility in a radical form is, according to the Epistle to the Philippians, the condition for exaltation both of Jesus and of those who are 'in him':

> Therefore God also highly exalted him
> and gave him the name
> that is above every name,
> so that at the name of Jesus
> every knee should bend,
> in heaven and on earth and under the earth,
> and every tongue confess
> that Jesus Christ is Lord,
> to the glory of God the Father.[11]

This passage from Philippians is prefaced by an injunction to follow the example of the voluntary humiliation of Jesus Christ.

Jesus also taught that the meek, not the proud, are blessed. And, quite remarkably, when he is addressed as 'good Master' Jesus responds, 'Why do you call me good? No one is good except God alone.'[12] Even Jesus must not rely on, or be proud of, his own goodness or virtue. Indeed most of

---

10   Philippians 2.6–8 REB.
11   Philippians 2, 9–11 REB.
12   Mark 10.18. Cf. Matthew 19.17 and Luke 18.19 (REB).

the Christian saints down the ages are remarkable for their unawareness of the goodness or holiness that others see in them. They themselves are more than usually aware of their sinfulness and failure; they do not regard themselves as people of virtue but as forgiven sinners, dependent on God, who live by grace rather than moral achievement, and therefore unselfconsciously show the virtue of humility.

In the New Testament, believers are frequently called upon to 'humble themselves', to serve the Lord in 'all humility of mind'.[13] In this freely chosen humility they are following the pattern of the incarnation, and claiming the promise that God will put down the mighty and exalt the humble and meek.[14] The Christian emphasis on humility was powerfully reinforced by the debate between Jesus and the Pharisees. The central charge against the Pharisees was that they became proud through their confidence that they were observing the law; they 'trusted in their own righteousness', or virtue. Jesus' teaching in this regard is aptly summarized in his parable of the Pharisee and the publican:

> He also told this parable to some who trusted in themselves that they were righteous and regarded others with contempt: Two men went up to the temple to pray, one a Pharisee and the other a tax-collector. The Pharisee, standing by himself, was praying thus, 'God I thank you that I am not like other people: thieves, rogues, adulterers, or even like this tax-collector. I fast twice a week; I give a tenth of all my income.' But the tax-collector, standing far off, would not even look up to heaven, but was beating his breast and saying, 'God, be merciful to me, a sinner!' I tell you, this man went down to his home justified rather than the other, for all who exalt themselves shall be humbled, but all who humble themselves will be exalted.[15]

Thus, from early days, Christians affirmed humility as a central virtue, perhaps the crucial virtue. 'The foundation of our philosophy,' wrote Chrysostom, 'is humility', and Augustine declared: 'As the orator, when asked what is the first precept in eloquence, answered Delivery; what is the second? Delivery; what the third? Delivery; so, if you ask me in regard to the precepts of the gospel, I will answer first, second and third, Humility'.[16] Aquinas quotes Gregory as saying, 'he who gathers other virtues without humility is like the one who carries straw in a high wind'.[17] This humility is

---

13 Acts 20.19. The word used here is *tapeinophrosune* – lowliness of mind. Cf. Colossians 2.18 and 23, 3.12; I Peter 5.5.
14 Luke 1.52, 14.11, 18.4 and 24.
15 Luke 18.9–14.
16 Augustine, *Letters* 118, in Carol Harrison (2000), *Augustine: Christian Truth and Fractured Humanity*, Oxford: OUP, p.35.
17 Thomas Aquinas (1969), *Summa Theologiae*, vol. 23: Virtue (1a2ae.55–67), Blackfriars, p.123.

certainly not an aristocratic or a military virtue in the classical sense, although it was often argued that soldiers could, and should, display the Christian virtues, including humility. Centurions, according to the New Testament, can be God-fearing and virtuous, but they must not embrace pagan warrior ethics. Humility puts ordinary people as it were in a privileged position over against the powerful and warriors.[18] Furthermore the emphasis on humility suggests that we should not rely on the strength of our bodies, the goodness of our actions, or the nobility of our character – on our virtue, as classically understood – but on the grace and forgiveness of God. For Christians, virtue is 'as much a gift as an achievement'.[19]

   Aquinas directly juxtaposes his treatments of pride and of humility. Pride is, for him, 'a mortal sin'.[20] It 'is always contrary to the love of God, inasmuch as the proud man does not subject himself to the Divine Truth as he ought'.[21] Humility, on the other hand is often regarded by Christians as the greatest of the virtues, although Thomas gives priority to charity or love as the 'form' of all the virtues, for it directs them to their proper end.[22]

   For Christians, humility before God and before people, including one's antagonists, becomes a major public as well as ecclesiastical virtue.[23] But it is perhaps not so much a virtue as a gift or a grace. And obedience, which hardly figured among the heroic virtues of the classical world, except for slaves and the lowest ranks of civil society, now bulked large. In most normal situations Christians were expected to obey their rulers, who were set over them by God. But obedience to God had priority: 'We must obey God rather than man,' declared the apostle.[24] And in a fallen world, where people, especially those in positions of authority, perforce had sometimes to

---

18   Alastair MacIntyre, *After Virtue*, p.170: 'the New Testament not only praises virtues of which Aristotle knows nothing – faith, hope and love – and says nothing about virtues such as *phronesis* which are crucial for Aristotle, but it praises one quality as a virtue which Aristotle seems to count as one of the vices relative to magnanimity, namely humility. Moreover, since the New Testament quite clearly sees the rich as destined for the pains of Hell, it is clear that the key virtues cannot be available to them; yet they are available to slaves'.

19   S. Hauerwas (1967), 'Virtue', in *A New Dictionary of Christian Ethics*, London: SCM Press.

20   St Thomas Aquinas (1973), *'The Summa Theologica' of St Thomas Aquinas*, vol. 13 (Second Part of the Second Part, QQ. CXLI–CLXX), London: Burns Oates and Washbourne, p.244.

21   Ibid., p.245.

22   See also Stanley Hauerwas and Charles Pinches (1997), *Christians Among the Virtues: Theological Conversations with Ancient and Modern Ethics*, Notre Dame: University of Notre Dame Press, esp. pp.27, 93, 143.

23   For a treatment of humility in conflict resolution, see Mark Gopin (2000), *Between Eden and Armageddon: The Future of World Religions, Violence and Peacemaking*, Oxford: Oxford University Press, pp.151ff.

24   Acts 5.29.

do things which they knew were no more than the lesser evil, or sinful acts which were nonetheless necessary, more than virtue ethics was required. Rulers and magistrates and ordinary folk as well had to learn both to struggle to be virtuous and to acknowledge humbly before God their failures, and seek forgiveness. For the virtuous person was now recognized as a humble person who could balance competing claims and operate prudently and modestly in the midst of the ambiguities and uncertainties of public life. In many situations the necessity of compromise had now to be recognized, along with the recognition that some necessary compromises were nonetheless sinful.

Virtue and Violence

It is, I think, too simple to say, with Stanley Hauerwas, that Christians and the Church have radically different understandings of the virtues from those dominant in the broader culture and society. There are, it is true, areas where a Christian understanding of the virtues is highly distinctive, but throughout history Christian and 'secular' understandings of virtue tend to interact with one another. And usually it has been held to be important that Christian accounts of the virtues are not confined to the believing community; they claim to be true and valid for everyone and for the broader society as well. The centrality of the virtue of humility, like the whole moral orientation of the early Church, points towards non-violence and something like what today would be called pacifism as a normal expression of humility. Peacemakers are declared blessed. The humble person turns the other cheek when attacked, verbally or physically. Reconciliation, the peaceful resolution of conflicts and disagreements, and virtuous (or holy) living demand humility rather than pride. We are even enjoined to be humble and modest enough to love our enemies, what Desmond Tutu calls 'the difficult but ultimately rewarding path of destroying enemies by turning them into friends'.[25]

As the early Church moved towards the Constantinian settlement, it became more and more difficult to maintain a consistent non-violent witness, and there had to be some rapprochement between the Christian virtues and the more military and aristocratic virtues of the Empire, the virtues that relate specifically to the deployment of power.[26] In Islam these issues were there from the beginning, because, as it has been aptly said,

---

25 Desmond Tutu (1999), *No Future Without Forgiveness*, London: Rider, p.138.

26 It is important to remember that this process is already taking place in the gospels and the New Testament Church. Jesus, for instance, commends the virtuous centurion, saying 'I have not found such faith in Israel' (Luke 7.9).

Muhammad was both Prophet and 'Islam's Constantine'. The story here is long and complex, and I wish to suggest that there was seldom an unqualified Christian acceptance of the classical virtues and the values of a state founded on coercion and violence. Rather the attempt was to tame and constrain the military and aristocratic virtues, and harness them to Christian purposes – to 'humiliate' them would not perhaps be going too far.

Humility and the other Christian virtues are not only concerned with the private and domestic sphere. They are of huge and continuing importance in public life. In the next chapter I shall explore a variety of endeavours to incarnate Christian virtue in public life, particularly the saintly idiom in politics, and the virtues of the martyr, and the holy warrior or crusader. Meanwhile I instance the continuing political relevance of the Christian virtues, especially humility in the work of that remarkable American public theologian, Reinhold Niebuhr. He constantly called for public humility, as in words written in 1947, in the early days of the Cold War:

> The best chance of our own powerful nation meeting the great responsibilities of which history has given us too brief a preparation, lies in abjuring every temptation to regard our power and our favoured position among the nations as proof of our superior virtue; and in listening patiently to the mounting criticism of our life (even though envy may partly prompt it) in the hope that it may make us wiser in the exercise of our power and more prudent in the discharge of our responsibility.[27]

These words are still deeply relevant in this time of terror in the early twenty-first century. Central to Niebuhr's public theology was the danger of the central sin of pride distorting political judgment and leading to imprudent and destructive courses of action.[28] 'Moral pride,' he writes, 'is the pretension of finite man that his highly conditioned virtue is the final righteousness, and that his very relative moral standards are absolute. Moral pride thus makes virtue the very vehicle of sin.'[29] Public life, to this way of thinking, should be seen as a sphere of humble service, or 'ministry' in the original sense. Niebuhr would agree, that is, with one of his most strenuous critics, John Howard Yoder, that what is at issue here is servanthood rather than status, recognition or reward. The politician should always beware of serving his own interests, or giving too high a status to his own judgments.

---

27 Reinhold Niebuhr (1947), 'America's Precarious Eminence', *The Virginia Quarterly Review* (Autumn 1947), p.490. I am indebted for this quotation and for my whole understanding of the role of humility in Niebuhr's thought to Dennis Lambert's splendid PhD thesis.

28 See Reinhold Niebuhr (1941, 1943), *The Nature and Destiny of Man*, London: Nisbet, vol. I, *Human Nature*, pp.198–242 for Niebuhr's classic account of pride as the central sin in public life.

29 Niebuhr, *The Nature and Destiny of Man*, vol. 1, p.212.

For the politician, too, is a sinner, apt to exalt unpleasant but necessary actions into divinely sanctioned causes. But the politician is called by God to be a servant, a minister.

Niebuhr's re-emphasizing of the traditional stress on the sinfulness of pride and the need for humility has been vigorously attacked by a number of feminist theologians. I think on the whole they accuse Niebuhr wrongly of attacking self-respect, or an appropriate *amour propre*. He is not advocating self-abasement, or the denial of one's own worth, nor is he supporting an *enforced* humiliation. These things make it difficult to enter into loving relationships, or authentic and caring community. Niebuhr is particularly focused on the dangers of pride among those of power and influence who take decisions on behalf of others. Indeed he sees humility as a grace, something given, rather than as an achievement, or something adopted under pressure. But pride is not, surely, as Daphne Hampson suggests, 'a peculiarly male temptation'.[30] Yet perhaps, with politicians like Margaret Thatcher and Indira Gandhi in mind, we might suggest that it is a special temptation to those in public life, of either gender.

Humility, in Arthur Schlesinger's words, 'must temper, not sever, the nerve of action'.[31] And so I now turn to the examination of some of the ways which have been used, and which continue to be used, to temper and constrain 'the nerve of action' with something like humility.

---

30 Daphne Hampson (1986), 'Reinhold Niebuhr on Sin: A Critique', in Richard Harries (ed.), *Reinhold Niebuhr and the Issues of Our Time*, London: Mowbray, p.47. See also Judith Plaskow (1980), *Sex, Sin and Grace: Women's Experience and the Theologies of Reinhold Niebuhr and Paul Tillich*, Lanham: University Press of America; Averil Cameron (1999), 'On the Grace of Humility', *Theology*, March/April 1999, pp.97–104.

31 In Charles C. Brown (1992), *Niebuhr and His Age*, Philadelphia: Trinity Press, p.vii.

Chapter 7

Virtues in Conflict

From the beginnings of Christianity and down the centuries there was, as we have seen in the previous chapter, a continuing debate about saints, heroes and martyrs, models of virtue in the public sphere, a debate which has suddenly become urgently relevant again today. This was in part the conflict between classical and heroic understandings of virtue and what the Church tries to teach about the proper life for human beings.

Two points deserve attention right at the start. In the first place, for Christians the model to emulate was the saint rather than the hero. The saint represented holiness rather than virtue or moral achievement. The saint characteristically regards herself as a sinner, but a forgiven sinner, and any righteousness she may possess is an 'alien righteousness', to borrow Luther's telling phrase. This righteousness is a gift from outside, not an accomplishment of which we may be proud. The saint trusts in God's grace and forgiveness rather than her own moral achievement, her own goodness. This is important not only for the saints, for the models we should seek to emulate, but for all Christians, and especially perhaps for those who, in positions of responsibility for others, are obliged from time to time to do acts which they know to be sinful, to be evil, even if they are commonly, one hopes, the lesser evil. Dietrich Bonhoeffer, the theologian taking part in the plot to assassinate Hitler knowing that it conflicted directly with the commandment against killing, is a case in point. And there are many others.

The second point is this: as we have seen, from the beginnings of Christianity, humility modelled on the humility of the incarnation, not pride, was the central virtue for Christians. And this raised constant questions about the use of power, force and violence, and how they might be constrained and controlled and channelled in a positive direction, even in a broken, sinful world.

Chivalry

Consider, for instance, the case of 'chivalry', in which the warrior was understood as following a distinctively Christian vocation, and only using violence in a chastened and strictly limited way for the defence of the weak or the establishment of justice. Chivalry drew heavily from the classical ideal of the virtuous warrior hero, but this was constantly challenged, enriched and modified by the Christian saintly tradition, as the two understandings engaged with one another down the years.

A splendid example of chivalry is Chaucer's 'true and perfect gentle-knight', who had 'jousted for our faith', and also served the Bey of Balat in battle against another 'heathen Turk'. He had fought all over the known world, and he was one who from the beginning had followed chivalry, 'truth, honour, generous thought and courtesy'. Everywhere, 'as well in Christian as in heathen places' he had been honoured for his graciousness. 'In his bearing modest as a maid', he was 'a true, a perfect gentle-knight.'[1] Chivalry was an attempt to Christianize what was regarded as the limited and necessary use of violence, and to constrain spirals of revenge and cruelty by setting before the warrior the protection of the weak as the great goal. Chivalry was in fact a coherent package of virtues which was in a way a compromise between the Christian and the heroic. It was an attempt to control and channel violence towards good, or less evil, goals. Soldiering was now recognized as a Christian and religious vocation. Dedicated Christian knights could belong to religious, quasi-monastic orders.

A process not dissimilar to the development of chivalry can be seen in some of the Icelandic sagas. In a Nordic society in which the *berserk*, who fought with maniacal fury, was regarded as a virtuous warrior, sure to reach Valhalla, the Christian monks who wrote down and transcribed the sagas implanted Christian values as they understood them in stories which had their origin in Nordic paganism a couple of centuries before they were written down. These stories in their original form relished the heroic and violent Nordic virtues, with virtuous warriors being sustained in battle by the hope of Valhalla.

Njal's Saga, for instance, depicts the coming of Christianity to Iceland as in large part a conflict between two understandings of virtue, regarded as a kind of duel between Thor and Christ. This was not seen as a simple conflict between humility and pride, however, for both sides had frequent recourse to glorified violence, despite the introduction of the concept of martyrdom in, for instance, the case of Saint Magnus. Out of the Norse berserk tradition that glorified violence there emerged Magnus, who refused to fight at the Battle of the Menai Straits and instead sang psalms in a loud voice, to the understandable fury of his embattled colleagues. He became a much admired Earl of Orkney, and was treacherously killed on the island

---

1   Geoffrey Chaucer (1951), *The Canterbury Tales*, trans. Neville Coghill, Harmondsworth: Penguin, pp.26–7; my italics.

of Egilsay, a politically inspired murder which was quickly depicted as a martyrdom. The Orkneyinga Saga sings his praises:

> St Magnus, Earl of Orkney, was a man of extraordinary distinction, tall, with a fine, intelligent look about him. He was a man of strict virtue, successful in war, wise, eloquent, generous and magnanimous, open-handed with money, sound with advice and altogether the most popular of men. He was gentle and agreeable when talking to men of wisdom and goodwill, but severe and uncompromising towards thieves and vikings, putting to death most of the men who plundered the farms and other parts of the earldom. He had murderers and robbers arrested, and punished the rich no less than the poor for their robberies, raids and other transgressions. His judgements were never biased, for he believed divine justice to be more important than social distinctions. While he was the most generous of men to chieftains and others in powerful positions, he always gave the greatest comfort to the poor. He lived according to God's commandments, mortifying his flesh through an exemplary life in many ways which, though revealed to God, remained hidden from the sight of men.[2]

Another exemplar of the Christianization of the Nordic understanding of virtue was Kjartan, the very model of the Viking Christian military saint:

> He was the most handsome man ever to have been born in Iceland. He had a striking face, with regular features, beautiful eyes, and a fair complexion. His hair was long, and fine as silk, falling in curls. He was tall and strong ... Kjartan was better proportioned than any other man, and everyone who saw him marvelled at him; he was better skilled in arms than most, extremely dextrous, and exceptionally good at swimming. He surpassed all others in all accomplishments; yet he *was a man of great humility*, and so popular that everyone, man or child, loved him. He was cheerful by nature, and generous with money.[3]

A veritable David Beckham of his day, or an early exponent of nineteenth-century muscular Christianity! Or perhaps a virtuous hero in the classical mode, with a topdressing of Christian humility.

Chivalry as a project intended to Christianize the heroic virtues disintegrated in the course of the Crusades, which became holy wars in which humility and restraint had little place, for in a Manichaean world-view the battle was an unqualified contest between good and evil in which the protagonists of the good had nothing save cowardice to be humble and modest about. The military orders were explicitly Christian, and dedicated to the values of chivalry, but soon they became the core of armies which

---

2 Herman Palsson and Paul Edwards (trans.) (1981), *Orkneyinga Saga*, Harmondsworth: Penguin, pp.89–90.
3 Magnus Magnusson and Hermann Palsson (trans.) (1969), *Laxdaela Saga*, Harmondsworth: Penguin, pp. 109–10; my italics.

showed little sign of Christian virtue. The Crusades became in effect holy wars in which the old heroic virtues triumphed over humility and restraint. The great St Bernard, for example, called for a crusade in rousing and immoderate terms:

> And now, for our sins, the enemy of the Cross has begun to lift his sacrilegious head there, and to devastate with the sword that blessed land, the land of promise ... What are you doing, you mighty men of valour? What are you doing, you servants of the Cross? Will you cast holy things to dogs, pearls before swine? ... Gird yourselves therefore like men and take up arms with joy and zeal for your Christian name, in order to 'take *vengeance* on the heathen and curb the nations'. Now, O mighty soldiers, O men of war, you have a *cause for which you can fight without danger to your souls; a cause in which to conquer is glorious and for which to die is gain.*[4]

Bernard was suggesting that holy warriors could find forgiveness in and through fighting for the holy places, rather than seeking forgiveness for fighting.

Thus 'furious religion' triumphed over Christian restraint again and again, as when in 1452 under the so-called 'Padroado Real', the Pope gave King Alphonso I of Portugal authority to 'wage war against Saracens, infidels, unbelievers and all other enemies of Christ, whomsoever and wheresoever they be' with the accompanying right to 'invade, occupy, seize and subdue their kingdoms', taking over their belongings, all 'for the greater glory of the divine Name'.[5]

The virtues of chivalry again and again slipped easily and remorselessly into a renewed glorification of violence, and the granting of a kind of Christian legitimacy to 'Holy Wars', in which Christianity as a 'furious religion' appeared to give unqualified authorization to total war, terror and the horrendous pursuit of national, group or personal self-interest. The tradition of chivalry lingers on, however, particularly among the military. For instance, in the last stages of the first Gulf War, Colin Powell declared that to allow a victory to turn into a massacre would be 'unAmerican and unchivalrous'. Furthermore there was, he said, to be no '*unnecessary* loss of American or Iraqi youngsters'.[6] Thus the Christian tradition of chivalry played a significant role in the development of just war thinking and the associated constraints, as I will discuss later on.

---

4   Arthur F. Holmes (1975), *War and Christian Ethics*, Grand Rapids: Baker Book House, p.89; my italics.

5   Cited by Penelope Carson in Robert E. Frykenberg (ed.) (2003), *Christians and Missionaries in India*, Grand Rapids: Eerdmans, p.135.

6   BBC television programme, 'The Gulf War', broadcast 1993/4.

Martyrs and Heroes

> The terrorist [according to a Russian nineteenth-century account] is noble, terrible, irresistibly fascinating for he combines in himself the two sublimities of human grandeur: the martyr and the hero ... He knows he is consecrated to death. He goes forth to meet it fearlessly, and can die without flinching, not like a Christian of old, but like a warrior accustomed to look death in the face.[7]

On the BBC programme *Newsnight* some time ago, a radical Muslim leader, Yusuf al Qaradawi, supported suicide bombing, declaring, 'This is not suicide; it is martyrdom in the name of God ... I consider this type of martyrdom operation is an indication of the justice of Allah Almighty.' He then developed his point, declaring that, 'If the Iraqis can confront the enemy, there is no need for these acts of martyrdom. If they don't have the means, acts of martyrdom are allowed. Allah is just through his infinite wisdom. He has given the weak what the strong do not possess and that is the ability to turn their bodies into bombs like the Palestinians, etc.'

Theologians and religious people need today to explore and examine such apparently horrifying religious legitimation of suicide bombing. Is suicide bombing ever an expression of virtue, an authentic act of martyrdom, witnessing to the truth of God, as Yusuf al Qaradawi affirms? Or is it fatally flawed as a way of witnessing to the truth of God?

Al Qaradawi uses a line of argument that is examined by Michael Ignatieff in his Gifford Lectures.[8] In asymmetrical conflict, the argument runs, 'the weak must have the right to fight dirty; otherwise the strong will always win ... In order to overcome the greater evil of injustice and oppression, the weak must be entitled to resort to the lesser evil of terrorist violence'. In the wake of 9/11, Arno J. Mayer declared, 'in modern times, acts of individual terror have been the weapon of the weak and the poor, while acts of state and economic terror have been the weapons of the strong'.[9] Ignatieff contests this argument on the grounds that there are clear and generally agreed moral rules governing the use of violence, and 'those who observe such rules deserve the name of freedom fighters. Those who do not are terrorists'. But that is not the end of the discussion. We still have to ask why people act as terrorists, and whether those who do such things

---

7 Serge Stepniak-Kravchinski (1883), *Underground Russia*, cited in Charles Townshend (2002), *Terrorism: A Very Short Introduction*, Oxford: Oxford University Press.

8 Michael Ignatieff (2003), *The Lesser Evil: Political Ethics in an Age of Terror*, January, Lecture 2: 'The Strength of the Weak: How Terrorism is Justified'.

9 Cited in Naim Ateek (2004), *Suicide Bombers: What is theologically and morally wrong with suicide bombings?*, Jerusalem: Sabeel Ecumenical Liberation Theology Centre, p.34. The article is also available in *Voices from the Third World*, **XXV** (1 & 2), December 2002, pp.121–50.

may be accounted heroes or saints – or martyrs, to use the term once again in vogue today.

For the early Christian Church the real heroes, the people of the greatest virtue, were not the soldiers, or the rulers, or the clergy, but the martyrs. They have a very special place in most Christian apocalyptic literature. They witness in their dying to God's truth and God's ultimate sovereignty. The faithfulness of the martyr testifies to God's ultimate ability to bring good out of evil, to give hope even in the midst of despair. 'Martyrdom,' writes Oliver O'Donovan, 'is not, in fact, a strategy for doing anything, but a testimony to God's faithfulness when there is nothing left to do.'[10] Martyrdom, however, is thus a matter of 'last resort'. A martyr is a witness to the truth, who puts her life on the line for the truth in which she believes. And the martyr who dies is often understood as one who absorbs in her suffering a little of the rage and terror of the enemy. Her dying as a martyr diverts some of the terror from the weak and the vulnerable. All this is a little after the fashion of the Lamb that has been slain in Revelation, and who has in dying neutralized at least some of the rage and violence of the enemy.

For Christians, Jesus' death on the cross was the prototypical martyrdom, and it is of the utmost importance to note that, on the cross, Jesus prayed to God, his Father, to forgive those who condemned, executed, betrayed or deserted him. This was indeed a strange victory. And for Christians the first martyr after Jesus himself was Stephen, who likewise forgave his enemies in his dying: He 'knelt down and cried out in a loud voice, "Lord, do not remember this sin against them". He said this, and died'.[11] And this martyrdom quickly became normative for the Christian understanding of martyrdom. St Fulgentius of Ruspe, for example, said of Stephen:

> And Stephen, so as to deserve to win the crown – which is what his name means – had love as his weapon and by it was everywhere victorious. Through the love of God he did not yield to the raging of the Jews, and through love of his neighbour he prayed for those who were stoning him. Through love he prayed for those who were in the wrong that they might be corrected. Through love he prayed for those who were stoning him to save them from punishment.[12]

In dying the martyr achieves a strange victory, for, in Tertullian's famous words, 'The blood of the martyrs is the seed of the Church.'[13] Martyrs

---

10   Oliver O'Donovan (2003), *The Just War Revisited*, Cambridge: Cambridge University Press, p.10.

11   Acts 6.59.

12   Fulgentius of Ruspe, *Sermon* 3.5–6, in *The Divine Office* 1, p.49*.

13   Tertullian, *Apologeticus* 50, Ante-Nicene Christian Library, Edinburgh: T. & T. Clark, 1869, vol. XL, p.138.

'desire to suffer ... in the way the soldier longs for war'. Tertullian continues:

> It is our battle to be summoned to your tribunals, that there, under fear of execution, we may battle for the truth ... This victory of ours gives us the glory of pleasing God, and the spoil of life eternal. *We conquer in dying; we go forth victorious at the very time we are subdued.*[14]

Among believers, martyrdom was to be welcomed, but not positively sought. 'You cannot win the martyr's crown by volunteering for it. You can only win it by witnessing and then taking the consequences,' writes Brian Wicker.[15] Martyrs are not suicides; indeed suicide is unitedly denounced by Christianity, Islam and Judaism. Yet martyrdom in the Book of Revelation is more than the passive and humble acceptance of suffering; the death of the martyrs affects for good the outcome of the battle.[16]

T.S. Eliot aligned himself with the dominant thrust of early Christianity when he depicted Becket as wrestling with the temptation positively to seek martyrdom, turning martyrdom into a kind of suicide, embracing humility in order to receive honour later on, doing the right thing for the wrong reasons, and thus changing the whole nature of the battle with sin and evil:

> Saint and Martyr rule from the tomb ...
> Think, Thomas, think of enemies dismayed,
> Creeping in penance, frightened of a shade;
> Think of pilgrims, standing in line
> Before the glittering jewelled shrine,
> From generation to generation
> Bending the knee in supplication,
> Think of the miracles, by God's grace,
> And think of your enemies, in another place.
> Seek the way of martyrdom,
> *Make yourself the lowest on earth,*
> *To be high in heaven.*[17]

Becket's temptation was much debated in the early Church, and the majority view was that martyrdom should be accepted, but not actively sought.[18]

---

14 Tertullian, *Apologeticus* 50; my italics.
15 Brian Wicker (2002), 'Conflict and Martyrdom after 11th September 2001', http://website.lineone.net/~ccadd/cta_paper_2002.htm.
16 I am indebted for this and several other points to my friend, Rev. Dr Paul Middleton.
17 T.S. Eliot (1968), *Murder in the Cathedral*, London: Faber and Faber, pp.40–42; italics mine.
18 But see Tertullian's letter *Ad Scapulam*, where he mentions the case when 'the whole Christians of the province, in one united band', presented themselves before the governor whose 'cruelty is our glory' demanding martyrdom.

Flight from persecution and probable martyrdom is disallowed by Tertullian,[19] but he would not and could not advocate suicide.

The idea of martyrdom in Islam came from Christian roots in the seventh century. Shia Islam in particular has at its heart the martyrdom of Imam Ali in 661, and his son, Imam Husayn, in 668. As a consequence the concept of martyrdom has a more central position in Islam than it has in Christianity. Martyrdom is generally understood as the offering of one's life in a *jihad*, or conflict with a just cause, and carries with it, as in Christianity, the promise of heavenly rewards. But in Islam from the beginning the emphasis was on death in battle with the infidel as witnessing to the truth, as martyrdom. Death in battle for Islam was not the only path to martyrdom and the joys of paradise, but it was the principal one, and Muslims who fell in battle with unbelievers were generally accounted martyrs, even if they had slain many before their own death. Islam, as a consequence, had far larger numbers of those who were entitled to the title 'martyr'. The contrast here with the Christian Church's reluctance to suggest that death in battle, even in a 'just war', is martyrdom is striking. There are, of course, Christian warrior saints who count as martyrs rather than simply heroes, but, even in these cases, the emphasis is on what they suffered for the truth rather than on military prowess.[20] Nor in early Christianity, as far as I can discern, is the killing, along with one's own suicide, of others, whether enemies or innocents, ever called martyrdom.

Political Martyrdom Today

The more recent understanding and practice of political martyrdom, especially in the Middle East, has a number of ominously distinctive features when compared with early Christian views of martyrdom. In both, martyrdom is regarded as a spiritual discipline which is a way of witnessing to truth. But these modern martyrs are in fact suicides: they are the agents of their own deaths and, furthermore, and very ominously, their intention in dying is to kill in spectacular destruction many of their enemies, not usually soldiers but ordinary citizens, men, women and children. Although martyrdom still has a framework of spirituality here, it has now become an agency of terror and of politics. The concept and the reality of martyrdom are put at the service of what can only be accounted terrorism. The

---

19   See Tertullian's *De fuga in Persecutione* in Ante-Nicene Christian Library, vol. XL.

20   I am indebted for the argument of this paragraph to Brian Wicker, 'Conflict and Martyrdom after 11th September 2001', http://website.lineone.net/~ccadd/ cta_paper_2002.htm and 'Martyrdom in Christianity and Islam', http://website. lineone.net/~ccadd/martyrdom_christianity.htm.

martyrs are recruited and trained; their actions fit into the grand designs of others.

And yet we must strive to understand what is happening before passing judgment. A television programme[21] on suicide bombers now in Israeli prisons was chilling to watch. For one thing, the young men and women involved were so ordinary and normal, like the kids next door.[22] It is too easy to suggest that they were simply puppets in the hands of others, being used for the advancing of purely political strategies. Their own explanations of their actions and their plans were almost entirely religious, although clearly more political motives were lurking behind and within the religious presentations. One said, 'We Palestinians prefer to die – we are hollow bodies leading a pointless life.' Another spoke of simple retaliation: 'As they kill us, we should kill them.' Only one spoke of hatred, suggesting it had been a dominating motive, but almost all explained and justified their actions in religious terms. Beforehand most of them – like those who hijacked the planes on 9/11 and flew them into the twin towers and the Pentagon – had had a period of spiritual preparation. They spoke of surrendering themselves to God, of martyrdom as leading to God and the assurance of paradise. 'The night before,' said one, 'I read the Qur'an and prayed. I knew I would soon become a martyr. That made me happy.' When questioned about the justification for killing the innocent a typical reply was 'It's God who kills, it's God's decision who dies.' Religion, it seemed, absolved them of responsibility for the consequences of their actions.

Research has shown that most suicide bombers are well-educated, middle-class people, not the impoverished. A forensic psychiatrist at Pennsylvania University, Marc Sageman, examined the profiles of nearly 400 people linked to al-Qaeda. He found that most are 'well-off, well-educated, middle-class, cosmopolitan, professional, married and sane'.[23] They are not wild psychotics, incapable of rational calculation, and driven by frenzy. Many of them have travelled abroad, often for education. Sageman comments, 'We are talking about the elite of the country sent abroad to study because the schools in Germany, France, England and the US are better.'[24] They know the world from personal experience, and this does not, apparently, modify their conviction that the US and the West generally is

---

21 BBC 2, transmitted on 10 November 2003.

22 'How can terrorists (who far from being 'criminals, crusaders and crazies' emerge in most good empirical studies as 'disturbingly normal' people) go out and kill innocent people in cold blood?', Charles Townshend (2002), *Terrorism: A Very Short Introduction*, Oxford: Oxford University Press, p.16.

23 Brendan O'Neill (2004), 'Terrorists: People who are just like us', *New Statesman*, 26 July, pp.16–17, drawing on Marc Sageman's book, *Understanding Terror Networks*, Philadelphia: University of Pennsylvania Press, 2004.

24 Quoted in O'Neill, 'Terrorists', p.17.

'the Great Satan' and that the state of Israel is demonic. In almost every way they are 'people like us', except perhaps that almost universally they take their religion very seriously and actually believe in paradise as welcoming to the faithful.

Why are these people 'in love with death'? At one level, they argue that they are at the receiving end of a 'war on terror' in which there is much indiscriminate killing of non-combatants, as always in war. The only difference, they believe, between their suicide bombings and the slaughter of non-combatants in Palestine by the Israeli army and in Iraq or Afghanistan by the occupying troops is that that they are denounced as terrorists while the soldiers who kill civilians as 'collateral damage' or by direct intent are often labelled heroes. In Naim Ateek's words:

> From the perspective of those who believe in and carry out the suicide operations, there is a simple and plain logic. As Israeli soldiers shell and kill Palestinians indiscriminately, Palestinian suicide bombers strap themselves with explosives and kill Israelis indiscriminately.[25]

It is clear that some suicide bombers are actively recruited, but most appear to be volunteers. Ateek suggests that recruitment is comparatively easy in Palestine: 'The desperate political situation makes it possible to have scores of candidates for "martyrdom". The preparatory stages are in effect accomplished by the Israeli army itself. It starts when these young people are traumatized, then brutalized, and eventually dehumanized by the impact of the occupation. Once they reach that stage, they become easy recruits.'[26] Ateek instances the father of a 25-year-old suicide bomber who attributed his son's action to 'humiliation and a broken heart'.[27] Suicide bombing seems to be the last, desperate weapon of the weak, seeking vengeance on their oppressors rather than calculating towards a possible political solution, and despairing of reconciliation.

But religion, and above all the promise of paradise to those who die defending the faith, provides the most significant rationale and justification of the martyr–suicide bombers. They are accounted martyrs (*shuhada*) witnessing to the truth and defending the community of the true faith.

But suicide bombers who accept the label 'martyr', and in their dying kill many innocents, are not witnesses to truth, either spiritual or political. Often they are recruited, trained and manipulated by malign and powerful terrorist organizations. Their action may express rage, despair, vengeance, 'furious religion', but is not congruent with the deep insights of the major faiths.

---

25   Naim Ateek (2004), *Suicide Bombers*, p.10.
26   Ateek, *Suicide Bombers*, p.33.
27   Ateek, *Suicide Bombers*, p.7.

Nor do they achieve a political objective, unless that is to provoke a disastrous spiral of escalating violence, as we see most clearly in the present impossible situation in Palestine/Israel.

Classical Christian martyrs gave their lives for what they believed to be true, to witness against lies and to save others. Martyrdom was a religious act which often had political consequences. The martyr witnessed to truth through personal vulnerability and courage. Martyrdom was, in a sense, witnessing to truth through vulnerability. Its courage was of a different order from that of the soldier. And there is still, surely, a prominent place in the public sphere for those who humbly witness to truth at the cost of security, promotion, or even life itself.

True Martyrs Today

The true virtue of the martyr in the public realm is as valid today as it has ever been. Vaclav Havel,[28] dissident and then President of the Czech Republic, in an essay written in 1978 and significantly titled, 'The Power of the Powerless', describes how quite ordinary people became dissidents, witnesses to the truth and often martyrs in the communist days in Czechoslovakia. Their little dissents radically shook the assumption that truth and power are one. Tiny protests gradually eroded the authority of the lie, and then became an earthquake. The powerless found power when they lived in truth.

Havel suggests that most of us are not witnessing to the truth, but living within the lie. Yet it is possible, even in a totalitarian dictatorship or under an oppressive empire, for individuals or groups to live in the truth, rejecting the lie, exploding the ideological justification of oppression by shouting that the emperor has no clothes on. The person who steps out of living within the lie (always a costly move) 'rejects the ritual and breaks the rules of the game. He discovers once again his suppressed identity and dignity. He gives his freedom a concrete significance'.[29] The truth is inherently a challenge to the system of lies. It involves a deep commitment to the priority of people over systems, any system. The task, Havel suggests, is dissent, resistance:

> It seems to me that all of us, East and West, face one fundamental task from which all else should follow. That task is one of resisting vigilantly, thoughtfully and attentively, but at the same time with total dedication, at every step and everywhere, the irrational momentum of anonymous, impersonal and inhuman power – the power of ideologies, systems, *apparat*, bureaucracy, artificial

---

28   Vaclav Havel (1987), *Living in Truth*, London: Faber.
29   Ibid., p.55.

languages and political slogans. We must resist their complex and wholly alienating pressure, whether it takes the form of consumption, advertising, repression, technology or cliché – all of which are blood brothers of fanaticism and the wellspring of totalitarian thought.[30]

Another modern martyr, Mahatma Gandhi, taught his followers that they must learn how to die for truth: 'Just as one must learn the art of killing in training for violence, so one must learn the art of dying in the training for non-violence.'[31] Dissent, resistance is the way to challenge the hegemony of lies, the way, perhaps the only way in a fallen world, to live in truth and witness to the truth, ultimately even in dying.

Christians – and Muslims – still believe that the truth is something to be lived and loved, and if necessary to die for. For Christians and indeed for Muslims, too, the example of Jesus, who voluntarily gave up his life for the sake of others, is a powerful beacon of guidance. The truth is not just a matter of thought, of ideas, of propositions. Havel was right to affirm that living in truth involves protest against lies and systems of untruth, and a profound witness to the priority of people over systems, of truth over slogans. It sometimes involves giving up one's life, but never the slaughter of multitudes of innocents. Martyrdom, Thomas Aquinas taught, is a gift and a calling from God, not an achievement of the individual.[32]

Martin Luther King Jnr, another modern martyr and witness to the truth, expressed both the necessity of escaping from cycles of violence, and the way of doing it when he said:

> The ultimate weakness of violence is that it is a descending spiral begetting the very thing it seeks to destroy. Instead of diminishing evil, it multiplies it. Through violence you may murder the liar, but you cannot murder the lie, nor establish the truth. Through violence you murder the hater, but you do not murder hate. In fact, violence only increases hate. Returning violence for violence multiplies violence, adding deeper darkness to a night already devoid of stars. Darkness cannot drive out darkness; only light can do that. Hate cannot drive out hate; only love can do that.[33]

We desperately need such modern martyrs if we are to find hope in today's violent world.

---

30   Ibid., p.153.
31   Cited in Brian Wicker, 'Conflict and Martyrdom after 11th September 2001' (http://website.lineone.net/~ccadd/cta_paper_2002.htm).
32   Cited in Wicker, p.5.
33   Martin Luther King, Jnr, from sermon preached at Eutaw Alabama Church in 1966, cited in Ateek, *Suicide Bombers*, p.24.

Chapter 8

Just War and Just Peacemaking

As Martin Luther King Jnr pointed out so forcefully, in a time of terror, violence tends to spiral out of control, constantly getting worse and destroying multitudes of innocent people, as well as losing sight of any sensible and achievable objectives, let alone looking to ways of resolving the initial disagreement and making peacemaking and the healing of old wounds more and more difficult. All the time the wounds get deeper, the rage sharper, and the possibilities of reconciliation more evanescent. Admiral Fisher represented a widely held view when, in criticizing the Hague Convention of 1899, he declared, 'The essence of war is violence. Moderation in war is imbecility. Hit first, hit hard, and hit everywhere.'[1] Apocalyptic theologies can, and often do, support this kind of attitude, and make things worse, especially if they persistently understand the world as the battlefield of Armageddon, the conflict between absolute good and absolute evil, the only outcome of which may be the total victory of the good and the elimination of the evil ones and all their works. It is important for Christians to remember that the Babe whose rocking cradle vexed two thousand years of history was – and is – also and primarily the Prince of Peace, and the Lamb who has already achieved through his life and death reconciliation, the One who on the cross prayed for forgiveness for his executioners.

If the goal is the realization of reconciliation and peace through forgiveness, it is not enough in such a time as today in a sinful world simply to nourish the peaceable virtues, important as that may be. Derrida noted the recent emphasis on the political significance of forgiveness as coming from the very heart of Abrahamic faith:

> In all the scenes of repentance, confession, forgiveness or apology which have multiplied on the geopolitical scene since the last war, and in an accelerated fashion in the last few years, one sees not only individuals but also entire communities, professional corporations, the representatives of ecclesiastical hierarchies, and heads of state ask for 'forgiveness'. They do this in an Abrahamic language which is not (in the case of Japan and Korea, for example) that of the dominant religion of their societies, but which has already become

---

1   Cited in Paul Gilbert (2003), *New Terror, New Wars*, Edinburgh: Edinburgh University Press, p.85.

the universal idiom of law, of politics, of the economy, or of diplomacy; at the same time the agent and the symptom of this internationalization.[2]

If forgiveness and reconciliation are for Christians the goals to be sought urgently and hopefully in situations of conflict, there is also a need for guidelines for the control of violence backed up if possible with effective sanctions. One such set of guidelines is to be found in the Christian tradition of the just war. This starts from the *lex talionis*: an eye, and no more than an eye, for an eye, and a tooth, and no more than a tooth, for a tooth.[3] This is intended to establish a kind of proportionality between the offence and the response, so that things do not spiral out of control and savage uncontrolled devastation follow. From this *lex talionis* there flowed a complex tradition of thinking on the just war and ways of limiting and ending outbreaks of violence and of terror as quickly as possible. Some of this has now become recognized in various protocols and as part of internationally recognized laws of war. And at times when decisions about conflicts and terror, and the use of violence and coercion, have to be taken, recourse is still commonly had to the riches of this tradition. Despite the fact that just war theory is often believed to apply only to wars between states, or well articulated organizations with a clear line of command and of accountability, the tradition is clearly concerned with constraining violence, even terrorism, where there is often great difficulty in identifying responsibility. After all, the *lex talionis* applied to conflicts at every level in a society or between communities. Its successor in 'just war' theory should be similarly wide in its bearing on the violent resolution of conflicts.

Christian just war thinking is a fairly continuous tradition of disciplined reflection on the use of violence, coercion and force in the resolution of conflicts. Its foundation is a recognition that the use of violence is deeply problematic, and for many Christian thinkers inherently sinful, although sometimes necessary in a fallen world. Aquinas and the other theological proponents of just war thinking started from a basic presumption against killing and war.[4] The just war tradition develops principles, standards or criteria to moderate, control and limit the use of violence, and bring a violent confrontation to as speedy an end as possible. Many of these criteria are also useful and appropriate in relation to non-violent ways of resolving disputes. Some of these just war criteria, like 'last resort', already suggest that violence is in most circumstances inferior to other means of resolving disputes, and that there should be a predisposition towards non-violence.

---

2   Jacques Derrida (2001), 'On Forgiveness', in *Cosmopolitanism and Forgiveness*, London: Routledge, p.28.

3   Leviticus 24.17–22.

4   Richard B. Miller (2002), 'Aquinas and the Presumption Against Killing and War', *The Journal of Religion*, pp.173–204.

Christian just war theory as a whole tends to urge that there should as soon as possible be a return to politics or diplomacy, or other non-violent means of resolution.[5]

This chapter is not a rerun of the pacifist–just warrior debate, in its classic form, or as reformulated in recent times by John Howard Yoder and Stanley Hauerwas. In many ways that debate down the years has been rather misconceived, and has forced many into excessively polarized and unbalanced positions, suggesting that the alternatives are either an almost cynical 'Christian realism' or an absolutist pacifism. My assumption is that, without necessarily embracing either of these extremes, Christians must take social and political conflicts, and those conflicts labelled 'terrorism', with the greatest seriousness and be passionate in seeking the best ways for their speedy and just resolution. Social, political, religious and economic conflict is not always avoidable, undesirable or unnecessary. But the way conflicts are handled and resolved should always be seen as of the greatest import- ance for Christians because it relates to the central stress in the gospel on reconciliation, and may have long-term implications for good or ill.

The predisposition towards non-violence that I have suggested does not mean that non-violent means of conflict resolution are necessarily and always in every situation superior in a Christian moral calculus to the use of force. Sometimes non-violent measures may actually prolong conflicts and leave deep wounds. Nevertheless there has been a steady reluctance to take non-violent and non-military methods of conflict resolution with the academic and practical seriousness that they deserve. Just war thinking can only be a part, if a central part, in a theology of conflict resolution. It itself points to the priority of non-military means. It treats the threshold of entry into violence with extreme seriousness, and the exit from violence as a door- way that should be gone through as soon as one can responsibly do so.

Just War Theory and its Limitations

In the Middle Ages, just war thinking was located squarely in a framework

---

5 The literature on the just war is, of course, immense, but I have been particularly influenced by Michael Walzer (1980), *Just and Unjust Wars: A Moral Argument with Historical Illustrations*, Harmondsworth: Penguin; Paul Ramsey (1968), *The Just War: Force and Political Responsibility*, Lanham: University Press of America; J.T. Johnson (1981), *Just War Tradition and the Restraint of War*, Princeton: Princeton University Press; Oliver O'Donovan (2003), *The Just War Revisited*, Cambridge: Cambridge University Press; by the writings of John Howard Yoder, particularly his debates with Karl Barth and Reinhold Niebuhr, and by recent American Roman Catholic discussions, particularly around the Pastoral Letters, *The Challenge of Peace: God's Promise and Our Response* (1983) and *The Harvest of Justice is Sown in Peace* (1994).

of Christian theological assumptions, central among which was often the conviction that violence is inherently and unavoidably sinful and evil, if sometimes, in a fallen world, inevitable, in the sense of being the only way to proceed. *Christian* just war thinking thus tended to take the sinfulness of active violence as axiomatic.[6] In a fallen world violence may occasionally be necessary, and the responsible statesman is under an obligation to use force for the defence of the nation. But violence remains sinful, a course of action that is not to be celebrated or lauded, but something that calls for repentance. Violence because of its sinfulness and destructiveness needs to be controlled and limited. It should only be used when all other possibilities have been explored without a satisfactory resolution of the conflict. Just war thinking thus seeks to *discipline* the use of violence and confine it within as narrow limits as possible. It is an attempt to transform violence as vengeance into violence as an effective, if dangerous, tool for the resolution of conflicts when all other possible ways have been tried unsuccessfully. The framework of just war theory is thus a predisposition against violence and in favour of non-violent ways of handling disputes. And beyond that it has as its *telos,* or goal, reconciliation. The only just intention in going to war is ultimate reconciliation and the restoration of peace.[7] Christians endeavour to relate the use of power and force in conflict resolution to the reconciling work of God in Christ. Violence remains theologically questionable even when exercised by a legitimate authority in a just cause, even when the various criteria of a just war are met, both *ius ad bellum* and *ius in bello*. As Oliver O'Donovan suggests, 'History knows of no just wars.'[8]

When this conviction as to the inherent questionableness, even sinfulness, and undesirability of the use of force even in a just war, even in police action, is lost, just war thinking easily degenerates into the justification, even sometimes the glorification, of war, violence and force, because it is assumed that, once the set criteria are met, the military action is no longer in any fundamental way questionable, deplorable or tragic. The secularization of just war thinking from the seventeenth century onwards in some ways seemed to simplify the whole issue. Now the tendency was to

---

6   Paul Gilbert suggests that Christian just war thinking is essentially 'punitive' rather than defensive and tends towards the justification of holy wars and crusades with little emphasis on limits. This is an extraordinarily one-sided reading of the Christian tradition, and particularly of Augustine. Indeed it was precisely against such Manichaean approaches to the justification of violence that the main Christian tradition rebelled. See Gilbert, *New Terror, New Wars*, pp.16–19.

7   On this, see especially Theodore R. Weber (2000), 'Vengeance Denied, Politics Affirmed: Applying the Criterion of "Just Intention"', in *Societas Ethica Jahresbericht*, pp.170–76, and (1989) 'Truth and Political Leadership', *Annual of the Society of Christian Ethics*, pp.5–19.

8   Oliver O'Donovan (2003), *The Just War Revisited*, Cambridge: Cambridge University Press, p.13.

suggest that war, or other acts of violence, were either just or unjust, and that was the end of the matter. One made careful and responsible calculations in accordance with the criteria offered by the just war tradition, and following this informed choice one's actions should leave one with a good conscience, and certainly no urgent and special need for penance.

But in actual situations of war and military conflict, such an approach is inadequate to the moral complexities and ambiguities involved. I remember, for example, the case of a British general, a professional military man and a committed Christian, who spoke some years ago on a BBC television programme on ethics in warfare. In the final stages of the Second World War, he said, he had been responsible for the safe crossing of the Rhine by a large contingent of allied troops. His advice from his intelligence was that the only way to guarantee the security of his men and a safe crossing of the river was to ask the RAF to 'take out' the historic city of Cleves. He knew Cleves to be crowded with refugee civilians as well as German troops and command centres. He agonized as long as he was able, and finally ordered the destruction of Cleves. Cleves was flattened by blanket bombing; the crossing of the Rhine was uneventful, but probably (certainty is rarely possible in such ethical calculations) this event made some contribution to the shortening of the war, and a reduction in the number of casualties. Yet, the general said, he still feels distress, guilt would perhaps be a better term, for the 'taking out' of Cleves. He still believed it was a *necessary* act, just according to the criteria of *ius in bello*, but it cannot be called *good*; rather it was something sinful but necessary, for which penance should be done, and forgiveness sought. Because of his Christian faith, the general was operating instinctively within an understanding of the just war which was within a theological frame which recognized guilt and spoke also of forgiveness and reconciliation.

Centuries earlier a similar theological ethics of war was expressed in the aftermath of the Battle of Hastings, when the Norman knights had to do penance for shedding human blood. They were fighting in a war declared by the Pope to be just, to set on the throne of England one who was recognized by the Pope as the rightful king. And yet, even in this context, violence was treated as sinful, and even 'just warriors' were driven back onto the forgiveness, mercy and grace of God.

Martin Luther, who in some moods was swashbuckling and bloodthirsty, declaring that 'the hand that wields this sword ands slays with it is then no more man's hand but God's, and it is not man but God, who hangs, tortures, beheads, slays and fights', made a similar point when he enjoined soldiers fighting in a just war of self-defence to pray, 'Dear Lord, you see that I have to go to war, though I would rather not. I do not trust, however, in the justice of my cause, but in your grace and mercy, for I know that if I were to rely on the justness of my cause, and were confident because of it, you would rightly let me fall as one whose fall was just, because I relied on my being right and not upon your sheer grace and mercy."[9] Luther's point is that we should not rely on the justice of our cause to win us acceptance with God. But the danger with this line of thought is that those set free and justified by faith seem, at least in some circumstances, free to act without restraint.

An adequate political ethics must be able to cope with the ambiguities of the 'real world', and respond not only to decisions and crises but also to their aftermath. It needs a theological framework which recognizes that sometimes we have to do things that are sinful but necessary. It needs to recognize and respond to guilt, and be able to speak of forgiveness and reconciliation not simply as the goal, but as present realities. Perhaps secularization of morals brought with it in relation to the ethics of war a narrowing and simplification which made modern secular just war ethics less capable of coping with the complexities and ambiguities of the real choices and decisions that have to be made, especially in a time of terror.

One of the things that has always puzzled me about just war thinking is that, for all its predisposition against violence, its determination to control and limit the legitimate use of force, and its concern to constrain and channel vengeance, it has remarkably little to say about alternative, non-violent ways of conflict resolution and about the ethical issues that relate to transitions from violence to diplomacy and 'normal' politics.

This chapter seeks to address some ethical issues that arise in relation to three areas of conflict resolution, issues that are rarely taken up by those who operate within the parameters of traditional just war thinking, but are urgently important in a time of terror.

- *The roots of violence.* What is it that leads to some conflicts quickly erupting into terror, whereas others can be resolved peacefully? Are there ways of nurturing and educating that discourage people from quick recourse to violence? Can the roots of violence in personality, social structure and collective memory be tackled and transformed?
- What about the moral significance of *moments of transition* from violence to non-violent processes of politics? Are not these moments of transition and how they are handled important as ways of avoiding spirals of violence and the accumulation of bitter memories which make violent outbursts in the future more likely and more bitter? Perhaps we need a kind of *ius ex bello*.
- Traditional just war thinking hardly touches upon *alternative modes of conflict resolution,* and the theological and ethical issues they raise. But

9　Martin Luther (1931), 'Whether Soldiers, too, can be Saved', in *Works of Martin Luther*, vol. V, Philadelphia: A.J. Holman Company, p.61.

particularly in a time of terror these ways of dealing with conflicts seem to be far more acceptable than the use of military force at a time when the devastating power of modern weaponry should give people additional cause for hesitation before launching into war. And certain just war criteria seem to be applicable to many non-military or non-violent ways of resolving conflicts. Perhaps we need to expand just *Thesis* war theory into just conflict resolution theory.

Education, Nurture and the Roots of Violence

Traditional just war thinking tends to assume that the conflicts with which it is primarily concerned arise entirely or mainly out of deep-seated conflicts of interest between nations, or quasi-national groups. The roots of conflict are thus understood as structural matters, to be resolved either through patient diplomacy or political action, or by the controlled use of force. This pattern does not easily fit a time of terror, when much violence is instigated by groups and organizations which often have a very unclear command structure and there is a good deal of confusion about objectives. Terrorist groups commonly are examples of 'furious religion' and are composed of angry people, with grievances, frustrations and sores which they believe are not being attended to or heard. Just war thinking tends to neglect the deep roots in personality, psychology and group dynamics of a tendency to turn, perhaps too easily, or as a last resort, to violence or to military force in the hope that it might resolve matters. Terrorist violence is usually rooted in a bitter resentment of injustice and oppression, real or imagined. And often enough terrorist groups have very vague or vastly ambitious objectives. The potentiality of social institutions such as the family, the Church or religious congregation and the school, which can and do instigate violence, to encourage instead peaceable resolution of conflicts and resist an easy recourse to violence is also frequently disregarded.[10]

It is a commonplace of social psychology that violence in the home makes it more likely that the children will be aggressive and prone to violence in later life. Cycles of violence often start in the domestic circle, and yet the family is the primary locale for moral education and the formation of character. In the family a child receives powerful messages and examples of the kinds of behaviour which are regarded as good and acceptable. Through being loved, we learn to love. Through being trusted

---

10   See Theodore M. Hesburgh, CSC (1993), 'Education for Peace-making' and Gordon C. Zahn (1993), 'The Challenge of Conscience', in Gerard F. Powers *et al.* (eds), *Peacemaking: Moral and Policy Challenges for a New World*, Washington, DC: United States Catholic Conference, pp.269–88.

we learn to trust. Through being treated reasonably and gently we learn how to handle anger, aggression and frustration. A violent family in which disagreements are met with violence, discipline is enforced with fear and children are intimidated is a breeding ground for violence in later life.

The educational system too can entrench or undercut lines of social division and suspicion – or strengthen them. The formal content of education is not the only, or the most important, part of the total educational experience. The environment, the way the school as a community operates, the human relations, the general atmosphere, the discipline of the school, the way disputes are resolved in school, the behaviour towards others that is encouraged are all important and influential parts of education. Sometimes the structure of education effectively denies its content, and forms pupils and their relationships in ways which are at odds with the declared aims of the system, tacitly encouraging misunderstanding of others and an openness to violence in the settlement of disputes.

The debate about the establishment by the World Council of Churches of its Programme to Overcome Violence illustrates the point I am making. The critics saw it as broad, ill-defined and overambitious. Thinkers like Ronald Preston rightly challenged the utopian sloganizing out of which it arose, like the Vancouver WCC Assembly's statement that 'without justice for all everywhere we shall never have peace anywhere'.[11] But the Programme, for all its excessive idealism, does endeavour to address the deep roots of violence, conflict and war in the life of nations, individuals, families and society, and indeed especially in churches. In doing this it is not taking up the classical pacifist stance, although it is influenced by the traditional peace churches whose witness is so influential in recent theology.

The WCC's Programme to Overcome Violence, as is appropriate for an ecumenical initiative, puts the role of the Church in the centre of its attention as a place where people should experience reconciliation and be encouraged to seek the non-violent resolution of disagreements. Churches, in their own inner life, and in their relations to one another, should provide a model of reconciliation, but in reality they are sometimes instigators of violence. Both the World Council of Churches and the Vatican have frequently spoken of the Church as the sign and sacrament of the coming unity of humankind. This is the calling of the Church, but it is painfully obvious that in many situations, especially perhaps in former dictatorships where civil society has been seriously eroded, the Church has become the guardian and expression of a rather chauvinist sense of national identity.

---

11   David Gill (ed.) (1983), *Gathered for Life: Official Report, VI Assembly of the World Council of Churches*, Geneva: WCC, p.132; Margot Kässmann (1998), *Overcoming Violence: The Challenge to the Churches in All Places*, Geneva: WCC.

Religion, almost any religion, can be a promoter of violence, yet today in this, as in other respects, both the Vatican and the World Council of Churches are playing an important role in summoning the churches to proclaim and to exemplify the Christian importance of reconciliation in the life of the world. Progress may be slow, but there has been progress in several areas.

The United Nations General Assembly proclaimed the years 2001–10 to be the 'International Decade for a Culture of Peace and Non-violence for the Children of the World'. This would emphasize the following:

- conflict resolution and respect for human rights in home and school,
- racial and economic justice, including the equitable distribution of global resources,
- the abolition of nuclear weapons and war,
- the spiritual roots of non-violence and compassion in all religions,
- the sanctity of all living things and ... the earth itself.

Unfortunately such noble aspirations, endorsed by every living Nobel Peace Prize holder, seems to have had little, if any, effect on what has turned out so far to be a notably violent period. Global aspirations need to be rooted in, and expressed through the local. And it is a little less difficult for the churches and similar bodies to do this than it is for the United Nations General Assembly because they have both local and global presence.[12]

Transitions from Violence

The transitions from armed force to non-violent means of dealing with conflicts that I wish to consider in this section are not only the changes that result from a victory, but the more subtle transitions that can take place when many people discover that violence is incapable of achieving their objectives.

I am not so much concerned with what one might call the Versailles or the Nuremberg ways of concluding a war, when in effect the victors determine the conditions for the restoration of peace, and the vanquished for a time at least are incapable of resisting the terms imposed on them by the victors. The victors seek redress, restitution, often revenge. At the Nuremberg trials, justice was seen as the infliction of their just deserts upon the perpetrators of atrocities and crimes against humanity on the defeated side. But this had little to do with reconciliation, forgiveness, the healing of

---

12   Robert L. Browning and Roy A. Reed (eds) (2004), *Forgiveness, Reconciliation and Moral Courage*, Grand Rapids: Eerdmans, pp.7, 198–9.

memories and the restoration of relationships. And atrocities on the part of the victors were hardly mentioned.

After the First World War the post-war settlement visited a punishment, believed by the victors to be just, upon the whole defeated population. The bitterness and recrimination which resulted fuelled the disputes which culminated in the Second World War. In neither situation was the process of the establishment of peace seen as primarily restorative, as oriented to the future, as concerned with healing relationships rather than settling past accounts. This way there was no easy escape from the cycle of recrimination, no healing of memories, little stress on penitence and forgiveness. The same issues arise today in relation to the absence of an 'exit strategy' from Iraq. How can an invading army that has destroyed a great deal of the infrastructure, killed many civilians and devastated such civil society as existed in Iraq expect to leave the country as a working democracy on the American model? Before such invasions, should the occupying powers not have had a clear and attainable list of objectives that are achievable by the limited use of force, after which the country is handed back to its people as a viable community?

I would like to reflect briefly on situations commonly labelled as arenas of terrorism, where neither side any longer believes it can win, and many people conclude that the continuation of military action makes the achievement of a good and happy resolution of the conflict less and less likely. The particularities of such situations vary widely, and it is difficult to generalize. But lessons can perhaps be learned from a brief discussion of two such situations in recent times: South Africa after the collapse of the apartheid regime, and Northern Ireland today.

In post-apartheid South Africa, where the ANC, commonly labelled a terrorist organization, is now the government, they have been attempting an alternative approach to peacemaking after their apartheid past, with all its atrocities and wounds and bitterness. They are using 'a different kind of justice',[13] which is restorative and healing, rooted both in Christian faith and in African tradition, and which sees justice as 'indispensable in the initial formation of political associations' with forgiveness as 'an essential servant of justice'.[14] They have been engaged in what Desmond Tutu calls 'the

---

13   The phrase is taken from an unpublished paper by the theologian Charles Villa-Vicencio, who was serving as Director of Research in the South African Truth and Reconciliation Commission. On the TRC, see Alex Boraine (2000), *A Country Unmasked*, Oxford: Oxford University Press; Richard A. Wilson (2001), *The Politics of Truth And Reconciliation in South Africa*, Cambridge: Cambridge University Press; and Nigel Biggar (ed.) (2001), *Burying the Past: Making Peace and Doing Justice After Civil Conflict*, Washington: Georgetown University Press.

14   Donald W. Shriver (1995), *An Ethic for Enemies: Forgiveness in Politics*, New York: Oxford University Press, p.6.

difficult but ultimately rewarding path of destroying enemies by turning them into friends'.[15] The issues of guilt and of retribution are not avoided or disguised, but they are put within a broader frame and a fuller understanding of justice and its end. The truth must be faced and moral responsibility accepted; the attitudes of the victims towards the perpetrators must be taken into account, for reconciliation is the ultimate aim. Perpetrators as well as victims need rehabilitation and healing. Justice and reconciliation rest on truth-telling, which is in itself often healing. Charles Villa-Vicencio explains the work of the Truth and Reconciliation Commission:

> Our task is to explain and to understand, making every effort to enter the mind of even the worst perpetrators – without allowing those who violate the norms of decency to escape the censure of society. Guilt rests not only with those who pull the trigger, but also with those who wink as it happens. It does, however, rest decidedly more with those who kill. The one who plots and designs death may well be more guilty than the person who pulls the trigger. The person, too terrified or even too indifferent to restrain the killer, is at the same time surely less guilty than the killer who may simply have followed orders. An appeal to superior orders or to due obedience is insufficient ground for claiming immunity – and the concern of the T[ruth and] R[econcilation] C[ommission] focuses clearly on those who gave the command to kill and those who did the killing – not on fearful bystanders or 'passive collaborators'. It would at the same time be a betrayal of history to suggest that they alone supported the evils of apartheid and its crimes. To fail to identify the extent of the evasion of moral responsibility for the failures of the past is to undermine the possibility of there emerging a moral fabric capable of sustaining a society within which the atrocities of the past shall never again occur.[16]

The Commission held hearings throughout the country under slogans such as 'Revealing is Healing', 'Truth the Road to Reconciliation' and 'The Truth Hurts, But Silence Kills',[17] inviting people to tell their stories and listen to the stories of others, for the healing of memories, for the redress of offences, for the overcoming of animosities and the lies that hostility engenders and, above all, quite consciously for reconciliation.

Where did this understanding of the need for a resolution that is healing, relational and restorative come from? Informed commentators are quite clear: it is derived directly from the depths of the Judaeo-Christian tradition, and finds significant affinities and resonances within African traditional culture and society. It seems therefore that theological insights have in this

---

15 Desmond Tutu (1999), *No Future Without Forgiveness*, London: Rider, p.138.
16 Villa-Vicencio, unpublished paper.
17 Desmond Tutu (1999), *No Future Without Forgiveness*, p.81.

transition at least been important factors in enabling a relatively undisturbed move from a situation of civil war to one of reconstruction, reconciliation and community building.

In South Africa there was an increasingly strong conviction that timing was of the essence. Back in 1986, the Kairos theologians had warned against the dangers of seeking an easy and premature reconciliation which was formal and ideal rather than real. According to Terence McCaughey, 'those who labour under the acutest sense of grievance, or who have simply suffered most, will recognise premature calls to reconciliation as a kind of impertinence'.[18] In South Africa many observers speak of moving from confrontation through transition to transformation, a long-drawn-out process, which needs to be handled with great wisdom and discernment because it is dealing with deep-seated conflicts of interest and understanding.

In some respects the 'troubles' and terrorism in Northern Ireland are similar to the conflicts about apartheid in South Africa. But the long history of oppression and injustice and the bitter memories of the past in Ireland run even deeper, and go back some five hundred years. There are memories in Ireland that call out for healing, and which must be healed before a settlement, reconciliation and justice become possible. There is truth, often painful truth, that has been hidden and which must be brought into the open, if wounds are to be healed. Timing, in situations such as this, is crucial. There must be a Kairos, an opportune moment, before trust and confidence and a new and broader, or perhaps more ambiguous, sense of identity can be built. And there also must be a change of goal, on both sides, changing from seeking victory in a 'war against terrorism', or retribution for ancient wrongs, to seeking reconciliation by way of forgiveness.

At the present time there may be such a long-drawn-out Kairos in Northern Ireland. This is partly because of a conviction which has spread slowly among all the main players that a lasting solution cannot be imposed by violence, and that military victory is impossible. This feeling has been strongly reinforced by a widespread weariness with the sufferings of civil war. Even the grassroots supporters of the paramilitaries appear to be insisting now that the cease-fire is observed, and that there is a move to political means of resolution of the underlying issues. The unproductive destructiveness of the violence of the Troubles is recognized by many as being a cul-de-sac. There is clearly a groundswell across both communities in favour of the approach of the Good Friday Agreement. And yet the whole process, even when handled with great sensitivity and generosity by

---

18   A. Morton (ed.) (1998), *A Turning Point in Ireland and Scotland? The Challenge to the Churches and to Theology Today*, Edinburgh: CTPI, p.36.

leadership on both sides, constantly teeters on the edge of breakdown because of the entail of bitterness and the slow and tenuous build-up of trust.

The Good Friday Agreement recognized the necessity of gradualness, of the slow building of confidence between those who have been for long enemies, of the tolerance within one province of two or more types of citizenship identity. The long-term future of Northern Ireland can be left open for a prolonged period of time, on the assumption that, as confidence and trust grow, it may be possible to move slowly towards an agreed long-term political settlement. This gives time, for healing, for the 'reconciliation of memories',[19] and for the steady gathering of support around a vision of the peaceable future of Northern Ireland. Such a vision may be articulated, commended and defended by politicians, academics, church and community leaders of integrity and imagination, such as Garrett Fitzgerald, the former Taoiseach of the Republic,[20] John Hume or David Trimble. Political and religious leaders, of course, cannot be simply visionaries; they need to be able to lead their people forward and retain the confidence of their constituencies of support. They must move, and move towards reconciliation, but they cannot go too fast if trust is to grow.

Both South Africa and Northern Ireland show in striking form the continuing importance not simply of religious rhetoric, but of central religious insights in non-violent conflict resolution, as there is a move away from violence to other, less harmful, ways of dealing with deep-seated conflicts. And these two examples raise important questions about the appropriate way of responding to terrorism.

Alternative Modes of Conflict Resolution

I would like to consider in this section two alternative modes of dealing with conflicts: Gandhi's *satyagraha*, which has emphatically religious roots, and has been labelled the 'saintly idiom' in politics and sanctions,[21] as used against South Africa in the days of apartheid, or against Iraq between the end of the Gulf War and the start of the invasion of Iraq ten years later. I then want to make some brief comments on recent initiatives in 'just peacemaking' and conflict resolution. *Satyagraha* was explained by Gandhi as follows:

---

19 On this see the essays in Alan D. Falconer and Joseph Liechty (eds) (1998), *Reconciling Memories*, Dublin: Columba.

20 See his paper in Centre for Theology and Public Issues, Occasional Paper 12, *Northern Ireland – A Challenge to Theology*, Edinburgh, 1987.

21 On Gandhi and his influence, see especially Peter D. Bishop (1981), *A Technique for Loving: Non-violence in Indian and Christian Traditions*, London: SCM.

It is a movement intended to replace methods of violence and a movement based entirely on truth. It is, as I have conceived it, an extension of the domestic law on the political field, and my experience has led me to the conclusion that that movement, and that alone, can rid India of the possibility of violence spreading throughout the length and breadth of the land, for the redress of grievances.[22]

Satyagraha rests on rigorous spiritual discipline. It 'laughs at the might of the tyrant and stultifies him by non-retaliation and non-retiral'.[23] It makes a sharp distinction between the evil and the evildoer. The evildoer, however vicious the wrongs committed, is still a fellow human being. A Satyagrahi 'must have a living faith in God',[24] 'must not harbour ill-will or bitterness' against the evildoer, and 'will always try to overcome evil by good, anger by love, untruth by truth, *himsa* by *ahimsa*'.[25] The means are believed to determine the end; violence seldom if ever leads to reconciliation.

In the Indian Independence Struggle, *Satyagraha* operated remarkably effectively as a kind of moral blackmail of the agents of the British Raj. It was a technique of appealing to the conscience and the reason of one's opponent by inviting suffering on oneself. The opponent, it is hoped, will be converted and become a friend and ally. The moral appeal to the heart and mind of the opponent is both more effective and more morally acceptable than the threat or exercise of violence. *Satyagraha*'s commitment to achieving independence with minimal violence and binding the diverse community together in the struggle had tremendous significance for the process of peaceful nation building in the newly independent Republic of India. *Satyagraha* also tackled, with some success, the purification of India from untouchability and the excesses of the caste system. It did not treat India as simply an innocent victim of imperialism; India too had to be purified, disciplined and renewed if it was to be fit for independence. It is not surprising that *Satyagraha* exercised great influence not only on the civil rights struggle in the United States, but on movements for independence throughout Africa and parts of Asia.

Yet even Gandhi himself recognized that there were situations where *Satyagraha* could not be effective. But for all that, *Satyagraha* should be recognized as an immensely significant non-military and non-violent way of resolving conflicts which leaves less entail of bitterness and hurt and enables reconciliation and nation building. It is effective in some situations but not in others.

---

22   M.K. Gandhi (1961), *Non-violent Resistance*, New York: Schocken, p.19.
23   Ibid., p.57.
24   Ibid., p.88.
25   Ibid., p.77.

2.   Sanctions have been much discussed and used in recent times as a non-violent or non-military way of resolving conflicts.[26] But sanctions may mean different things, and may be used for very different purposes. Economic sanctions may be used as a way of punishing or disabling an antagonist before or after military conflict, or in support of armed action. Sanctions may be a serious way of bringing economic and political pressure to bear on an antagonist to force him to give way or compromise, or at least to come to the negotiating table. On the other hand, some sanctions are important primarily for their symbolic value, as a way of making a dramatic statement of principle. Some people suggest that sanctions are by their nature morally preferable to the use of military force, and appropriate in almost all circumstances, but this is, I think, questionable. But perhaps just war criteria may be helpful in analysing some of the moral issues that can arise in the use of sanctions.

The sanctions deployed against apartheid South Africa were of various kinds. Boycotts of South African goods were sponsored by a variety of church and anti-apartheid groups, and encouraged by a number of prominent church leaders and others within South Africa. These boycotts had rather little direct economic impact on the South African economy, but they represented a powerful expression of solidarity, and offered many opportunities for education about the realities of apartheid. The impact within South Africa of the sport and cultural boycotts was far more considerable. These, while in themselves exercising little economic or political pressure, forced many South African Whites to ask why the rest of the world was so vehement in rejecting apartheid, and assured many South African Blacks that they had much support outside South Africa.

Disinvestment and the arms embargo had more direct political and economic consequences, and it has been argued that the economic pressure on South Africa was the single most important cause for the release of Nelson Mandela and the mounting recognition that apartheid could not be sustained. It was frequently argued at the time that the main victims of economic sanctions were South African Blacks, an argument that is essentially the just war prohibition of attacks on non-combatants. The fact that sanctions were called for and supported by Black leaders such as Desmond Tutu, who argued that Blacks were willing to make sacrifices and suffer if this brought the end of apartheid closer, did not mean that questions about 'targeting' were redundant. But, on the whole, sanctions against apartheid South Africa proved to be an effective and well directed mode of non-military action, which kept the door to reconciliation and

---

26   See especially Ray Pentland (2002), 'Just War – Just Sanctions', *Political Theology*, **2** (3), pp.178–95. Pentland applies just war criteria to the assessment of sanctions as a way of resolving conflicts, with special attention given to sanctions against Iraq.

peace more open than it would have been if apartheid had disintegrated in the face of military action internally and from outside.

The sanctions against Iraq following the first Gulf War were, of course, of a different order. They followed a destructive military action which, inasmuch as it successfully achieved its stated objective by repelling aggression against Kuwait, seemed to fit *ius ad bellum* criteria. The first Gulf War had serious continuing impact on the Iraqi civilian population through destruction of the infrastructure. Sanctions following the war were apparently aimed at objectives such as destroying Iraq's capacity to develop weapons of mass destruction and weakening the regime, but they were singularly and disgracefully ineffective in achieving their objectives. Inasmuch as their devastating effects were primarily on the civilian population, they would seem to fall foul of the principles of discrimination and non-combatant immunity. Indeed sanctions against Iraq, backed up as they were by frequent air strikes in support of the no-fly zones, looked like punishment of the people of Iraq rather than a responsible use of non-military means to achieve a political goal, in particular the restoration of peace in the region. If just intention means that the use of military or non-military means is only allowable to resolve a conflict and achieve peace and reconciliation, the sanctions against Iraq seemed to be highly questionable on moral grounds. Here sanctions appeared to be simply war carried on by other means, and perhaps without as close a moral scrutiny as armed conflict is accustomed to receive. Certainly sanctions against Iraq following its military defeat in 1991 seemed to be of a radically different moral order from sanctions against South Africa, aimed at supporting the ending of apartheid.[27]

Just Peacemaking[28]

It is much to be welcomed that a great deal of attention is being devoted today, not only to what makes a just peace, but to ways of encouraging mediation and negotiations to resolve deep-seated disputes and terrorism.[29] Glen Stassen and his colleagues have laid down 'Ten Practices of Just Peacemaking', which they are testing in situations of deeply entrenched

---

27   See Ray Pentland, 'Just War – Just Sanctions', esp. pp.184–92.

28   See especially, Glen H. Stassen (2004), 'Just Peacemaking as Hermeneutical Key: The Need for International Co-operation in Preventing Terrorism', *Journal of the Society of Christian Ethics*, **24** (2) pp.171–91.

29   See, for example, Glen H. Stassen (ed.) (1992), *Just Peacemaking: Transforming Initiatives for Justice and Peace*, Louisville: Westminster/John Knox, the essays and bibliography on Just Peacemaking in *Journal of the Society of Christian Ethics*, **23** (1), Spring/Summer 2003, or the work of the Department of Peace Studies at the University of Bradford.

conflict like the Balkans. In Stassen's book, David Steele outlines ten criteria for effective 'Co-operative Conflict Resolution'. These call for those involved to understand the perspectives and needs of their adversaries; to listen carefully before making judgments, to distinguish judgments about behaviour and actions from judgments about people or cultures; to acknowledge their own involvement in the creation of conflict; to be transparent and honest in all their dealings; to encourage partnership in problem solving; to use force only to create space for a non-violent solution; to be willing to take risks; to support long-term solutions; and to recognize justice and peace as being correlative to one another. Such guidelines or principles have, of course, a variety of roots, in common sense, theology and traditions of diplomacy, to name but a few.

One of the more important of such roots may be Jürgen Habermas's emphasis on communication, particularly his 'discourse ethics', and positing of an 'ideal speech situation' in which consensus may be achieved, and all the participants are free to speak their minds without intimidation, constraint, fear, threat or privileged discourses. Everyone who has an interest, or something relevant to say, should be entitled to participate in the discussion. Habermas admits that there is structural violence in most societies:

> We in the West do live in peaceful and well-to-do societies, and yet they contain a *structural* violence that, to a certain degree, we have gotten used to, i.e., unconscionable social inequality, degrading discrimination, pauperization, and marginalization.[30]

Terrorism, for Habermas, is a 'communicative pathology'. 'The spiral of violence,' he writes, 'begins as a spiral of distorted communication that leads through the spiral of uncontrolled mutual mistrust to the breakdown of communication'.[31] Where there is breakdown of communication, and the replacement of communication in more direct ways by acts of terror, there must be a process of healing, of restoration of honest communication and truth telling.

Accordingly people concerned with conflict resolution who not only hear words, but listen to people carefully and critically, are more likely, in dialogue with the people to whom they are attentive, to develop understandings of what peace may require in a particular context. In dialogue and in listening, relationship and community are built up and we discover together how conflicts may be resolved. According to John

---

30 Giovanni Borradori (2003), *Philosophy in a Time of Terror: Dialogues with Jürgen Habermas and Jacques Derrida*, Chicago: University of Chicago Press, p.63.

31 Ibid., p.64.

Forester, a planner much indebted to Habermas, in words which are more pressingly relevant today than when they were first written:

> Developing the ability to listen critically is a political necessity. Listening well is a skilled performance. It is political action, not simply a matter of a friendly smile and good intentions. Without real listening, not simply hearing, we cannot have a shared, critical and evolving political life together. In listening we may still better understand, explain, and cut through the pervasive 'can't', the subtle ideological distortions we so often face, including, of course, our own misunderstandings of who we are and may yet be. Listening well, we can act to nurture dialogue and criticism, to make genuine presence possible, to question and explore all that we may yet do and yet become.[32]

Real listening, especially in a time of terror, when the message may be deeply unwelcome, is not easy. But in the practice of peacemaking in face-to-face situations at least, Habermas's discourse ethics can be shown to 'work', and only so can people be brought together and held together in a just community; because for Habermas the *telos*, or goal, of speech and interaction is reaching understanding rather than asserting control.

David Schlosberg applied Habermas's theory of communicative action to conflict resolution in American cities. Such programmes in San Francisco were directed towards a just outcome from situations of conflict through what they called 'active listening', aimed at deeper understanding: 'As one participant put it, "the panel makes sure each disputant understands what the other is saying. Once there's mutual understanding, the first hints of conciliation usually begin to emerge".'[33] The success rate is remarkably high: 'For the two programmes examined ... in San Francisco and Santa Cruz, once people agree to participate disputes are conciliated in a mutually agreeable manner in over 95% of the cases.'[34]

Thus the procedures of discourse that Habermas proposes can provide a model for actual ways of achieving just outcomes from real conflict situations. Schlosberg's other case, of non-violent action in social agitation, suggests that these methods may be appropriate in wider circles than in face-to-face relationships. Leonard's examples see the approach of communicative action for justice as effective in broad social movements, mainly of critique and protest.[35] But it is not easy to see how communicative

---

32   John Forester (1989), *Planning in the Face of Power*, Berkeley: University of California Press, p.118.

33   David Schlosberg (1995), 'Communicative Action in Practice: Intersubjectivity and New Social Movements', *Political Studies*, **XLIII**, p.300.

34   Ibid., p.301.

35   See Stephen T. Leonard (1990), *Critical Theory in Political Practice*, Princeton: Princeton University Press.

action starts and develops in an age of terror, when both sides are determined to eliminate rather than listening to the other. Peacemaking has to be concerned with opening up authentic and truthful communication, even with the perpetrators of 9/11 and other atrocities. At this point Habermas and the principle of subsidiarity in Roman Catholic social teaching point in the same direction. But, just as the act of communication has implicit in it the *telos* of consensus and community, so Habermas's account holds up the rather utopian hope of a global broad community in which people attend to one another's feelings and listen to what they are saying and what they are afraid to say. Justice is what holds people freely and peaceably together in community; lurking in Habermas's account of the ideal speech situation is the hope of a reconciled community in which relationships are just and loving.

What has theology to say about non-military means of conflict resolution? The first and most emphatic point is to reaffirm the traditional predisposition against the use of violence, while recognizing with regret that in some circumstances the controlled use of force is the only way of dealing with evil. There is, next, the recognition that many of the limitations and constraints put by the tradition of just war thinking are in fact necessary also for all forms of non-military action to resolve conflicts. Non-military actions, like wars, can have diffuse or questionable objectives, have little likelihood of success, can have devastating effects on the civilian population, can easily go out of control and escalate into violence, or can be vindictive and vengeful.

That is why the controlling emphasis on the goals of reconciliation, the restoration of peace and the building of community are so vitally important. The means used should be coordinated with this goal, which comes straight from the heart of the theological tradition, and is one of the distinctive gifts that faith has to offer in a world that is full of terror and difficult conflicts, hard to resolve.

Epilogue: Forgiveness and Reconciliation

For Christians in a time of terror, reconciliation, the restoration of just and loving community, is the goal, and forgiveness is the way to that goal. And Christians further believe that the task is the full realization of a reconciliation which has been decisively defined, exemplified and achieved by and in the life and death of Jesus Christ. This Jesus taught his disciples to 'forgive and you will be forgiven', to pray 'forgive us our sins for we ourselves forgive everyone indebted to us', and to 'love your enemies [and] do good to those who hate you ... Do to others as you would have them do to you.'[1] And with these injunctions which flow from the gospel, believers have been given a task, entrusted with the ministry of reconciliation: God has reconciled us to himself in Christ and has given us the 'ministry of reconciliation'; that is, that in Christ God was 'reconciling the world [*kosmos*] to himself ... and entrusting the ministry of reconciliation to us.'[2] This ministry of reconciliation is not confined to the personal and spiritual spheres; it has universal import, because it lies at the heart of the Christian message and the life and work of Jesus.

Words from the Cross

St Luke recounts that Jesus, crucified between two notorious evildoers, hanging from the freshly erected cross on which he was to die, said, 'Father, forgive them, for they do not know what they are doing.'[3]

- This was the one whose disciples had slept while he wrestled in the Garden with his awesome destiny.
- This was the one who had been betrayed by one of his own inner circle.
- This was the one whose disciples and friends had for the most part deserted him.
- This was the one whose leading follower had publicly denied having anything to do with him.

---

1   Luke 6.37; 11.4; 6.27–31.
2   2 Corinthians 5.18–19.
3   Luke 23.34.

- This was the one for whose blood the mob had bayed, the very mob that five days before had welcomed him with waving palm branches and cries of 'Hosanna'.
- This was the one who had been denounced by the leaders of his own people and the guardians of the faith of Israel, who demanded his execution.
- This was the one who had been condemned unjustly, yet knowingly, by a craven Pilate, who attempted to wash his hands of the whole affair.
- This was the one who was mocked, degraded, humiliated by sadistic soldiers, who flogged and tortured him.
- This was the one who was forced to carry the weighty cross, the instrument of his own execution, to Golgotha, outside the city walls.
- This was the one who was nailed to the same cross, which was then slowly, painfully erected. He was left to die in excruciating pain, mocked and derided by the onlookers.

He was alone, in agony, raised up above the earth to die. Alone, that is, except for a few women and others who were there to be with him in his pain and aguish. We can understand the disciples' absence. We would do almost anything to avoid being present at such sadistic scenes of suffering and degradation and evil. And Jesus from the cross, in all his pain, and desolation, and fear said, 'Father, forgive them, for they do not know what they are doing.' Father, he prayed:

- Forgive the criminals dying beside me.
- Forgive the disciples who betrayed, denied, deserted me.
- Forgive the mob that bayed for my blood.
- Forgive the priests who arrested and condemned me.
- Forgive Pilate, who knowingly sent a just man to execution.
- Forgive the soldiers, sadists who tortured me, to get their kicks from inflicting pain.
- Forgive those who drove the nails into my hands.
- Forgive those who mocked me.

'Father, forgive them all, for they do not know what they are doing'. And if those wicked folk of long ago can be forgiven by God, so can folk of today:

- the terrorists,
- the suicide bombers,
- the torturers,
- the paedophiles,
- the abusers,

- the big-time cheats,
- and people like us, whose sins and failures are less spectacular, yet whose lives and whose relationships call out for forgiveness and for healing.

Something quite extraordinary, something of cosmic importance, was happening at that moment, when Jesus said, 'Father, forgive them, for they do not know what they are doing', something quite new in history. It was not just that Jesus was teaching and demonstrating the importance of the truth that forgiveness in our family and personal relationships is costly because it is healing. He was showing that forgiveness and reconciliation are of universal significance if community, care, joy and peace are to survive or be restored.

After a horrendous and unjust killing of an innocent and wonderful man, one would expect his followers to retaliate. An eye for an eye, a tooth for a tooth. But Jesus forbad vengeance. When one of his disciples produced a sword in the Garden and struck the High Priest's servant, Jesus rebuked him, saying, 'No more of this.' But vengeance, as we see today in Iraq, and Palestine and Israel, and Northern Ireland, and many another place, spirals easily out of control, leading to bloodbaths of the innocent, genocide in Rwanda, the Gulag in Stalin's Soviet Union, the massacre of Muslims in Srebrenica, torture and abuse of prisoners in Iraq, massive attacks on innocent civilians. One could go on.

Forgivenesss in Public

Karl Barth dramatically captured the centrality of forgiveness and reconciliation when, after the defeat of Hitler and the Nazis, the end of a conflict in which he himself had played no small role, he wrote, in 'A Speech of Christ addressed to the Germans':

> Come unto me, all you unpleasant ones, you bad Hitler boys and girls, you brutal SS soldiers, you wicked Gestapo scoundrels, you sad compromisers and collaborators, all you herds of people who have patiently and stupidly followed your so-called Führer! Come unto Me, you guilty ones and you accomplices, who now receive and have to receive what your deeds are worth! Come unto Me, I know you well but I do not ask who you are and what you have done. I only see that you are at the end of your rope and must start all over again whether you like it or not. I want to refresh you and precisely with you, I now want to start anew from the very bottom. I am for you! I am your friend!'[4]

---

4   Cited in Frank Jehle (2002), *Ever Against the Stream: The Politics of Karl Barth, 1906–1968*, Grand Rapids: Eerdmans, p.83.

'The discoverer of the role of forgiveness in the realm of human affairs,' declared Hannah Arendt, 'was Jesus of Nazareth.' She makes a very important point. But I do not think that, in her wonderful book, *The Human Condition*, she takes the full measure of the importance, and the costliness of the forgiveness which is exemplified and realized in these words from the cross, when Jesus sought and won forgiveness for all of us: 'Father, forgive them, for they do not know what they are doing.'

Forgiveness, as the faculty of being able to undo the effects of action, is essential if people are to be free agents, and able to make fresh starts, if the entail of past errors is to be erased, if the vicious circle of vengeance is to be overcome. Jesus, Hannah Arendt writes, denied that only God had the power to forgive sins, and insisted that there was a duty laid upon disciples to forgive without limit. She affirms that Christianity teaches that 'only love can forgive because only love is fully receptive to *who* somebody is, to the point of being always willing to forgive him whatever he may have done', and accordingly there is a problem in speaking about such loving forgiveness in the public sphere. What love is in face-to-face relations, respect is in the larger domain of human affairs, she suggests. But surely the manifestation of love in the public realm is justice rather than 'respect', and therefore we must speak of justice savoured with mercy and forgiveness.[5]

It is true that 'one cannot do other people's forgiving for them'.[6] Nor may a detached observer tell victims that they should forgive. The time and the situation must be right for forgiveness if it is not to be something cheap and superficial. God, as victim, offers forgiveness: 'On the cross Christ "bears" our sin, but this is not expiation. What happens there is the absorption of violence, the definition of power, and the establishment of the possibility of forgiveness.'[7] Human victims can mediate the divine forgiveness, and this forgiveness heals and establishes justice. Donald Shriver, in his remarkable book, *An Ethic for Enemies: Forgiveness in Politics*, argues that Black Americans have shown a remarkable openness to the possibility of forgiving their oppressors. Since Emancipation, if not before, the culture of a significant proportion of Black Americans, so deeply shaped by Christian faith, has given them 'a predisposition toward, an ingrained *gift* for, injecting forgiveness into their political relations with the white majority of this country'.[8] And in South Africa today it is not only Nelson Mandela but multitudes of ordinary Blacks who show a quite extraordinarily

5 Hannah Arendt (1958), *The Human Condition*, Chicago: University of Chicago Press, pp.236–43.

6 Peter Hinchliffe (1982), *Holiness in Politics*, London: Darton, Longman and Todd, p.198.

7 Timothy Gorringe (1996), *God's Just Vengeance: Crime, Violence and the Rhetoric of Salvation*, Cambridge: Cambridge University Press, p.247.

8 Donald Shriver (1995), *An Ethic for Enemies: Forgiveness in Politics*, New York: Oxford University Press, p.177.

magnanimous willingness to forgive, which provides the essential conditions for building a just nation. Kenneth Kaunda and Desmond Tutu both speak of forgiveness as the only way of overcoming 'the entail of the past', and Kaunda believes there is a special African gift for forgiveness. Yet if forgiveness is to be effective in politics it must be possible for governments, which are not victims, to speak a word of forgiveness. Especially in situations where the entail of history cannot be undone, where it is impossible for past injuries to be cured or full restitution to be made, justice can only be established through forgiveness and this forgiveness is itself a component of justice. It is as hard for collectivities to repent as it is for them to forgive, and there are not many instances of either happening. But without repentance and forgiveness the way to justice is closed.

× and if apology!

Forgiveness: Where Healing Begins[9]

Forgiveness is not forgetting, plastering over the cracks, pretending that nothing wrong has happened. Forgiveness is healing, and it leads to reconciliation. It was not easy for Jesus to claim God's forgiveness for his tormentors and betrayers. It is not easy for us to forgive, or to seek forgiveness. We all find it hard to say sorry. When we are threatened or challenged we want to hit back, to retaliate, but seeking and offering forgiveness is the only way to sustain a decent family, community, nation or world. For forgiveness based on recognition of the truth is healing, as ⫫ was found out in South Africa after apartheid through the work of the Truth and Reconciliation Commission.

Where do we start? Not, perhaps, with declarations from the United Nations, or actions by governments and huge NGOs. We start most certainly with individual acts of forgiveness, healing and reconciliation which begin to break up the log-jam of vengeance. What individuals who know they have been forgiven can do is important. It is more than important; it is crucial. For without such individual acts of generosity, forgiveness and healing reconciliation is impossible. And so I finish with two true stories, and a remarkable prayer. The first comes from Jonathan Sacks's wonderful book, *The Dignity of Difference*.

Laura Blumenfeld is a young American Jew. In 1986, her father, a rabbi, was visiting Jerusalem. While walking in the Old City he was shot by a Palestinian terrorist. The bullet missed his brain by half an inch. Seriously injured, he survived. His daughter, however, could not forget or forgive. Years later, by then

---

9   For a fuller, but now somewhat dated, treatment of forgiveness see chapter 10 of Duncan B. Forrester (1997), *Christian Justice and Public Policy*, Cambridge: Cambridge University Press.

a journalist, she travelled to Israel and, without disclosing her identity, befriended the family of the gunman and began a correspondence with the terrorist himself, now in jail. Not knowing that he was speaking to the victim's daughter, the father of the gunman explained why his son shot an American stranger: 'He did his duty. Every Palestinian must do it. Then there will be justice.' Another son added: 'My brother never met the man personally. It's not a personal issue. Nothing personal, so no revenge.' Laura wrote in her diary, 'The heat was rising in my face. It was personal. It was personal to me.'

She attends the terrorist's trial and persuades counsel – still without revealing who she is – to let her give testimony. On the witness stand she finally discloses the fact that she is the victim's daughter and that she has come to know the gunman and his family so that they can put a personal face to the family of the injured man and understand that there is no such thing as an impersonal victim of violence. In the middle of her cross-examination, she is interrupted by another voice:

A woman stood up at the back of the courtroom. She blurted out in English, in a loud, shaking voice, 'I forgive Omar for what he did.'

Forgive? It was my mother. This was not about forgiveness, didn't she understand? This was my revenge.

'And if the Blumenfeld family can forgive Omar,' my mother continued, 'it's time for the State of Israel to forgive him.'

The two women leave the court in tears, but the family of the gunman run after them and embrace. Later the gunman writes to Laura, 'We have been in a state of war and now we are passing through a new stage of historical reconciliation where there is no place for hatred and detestation.'[10]

Mary McAleese, the former President of Ireland, tells the story of Gordon Wilson:

It is a rare person who arrives at [a] state of perfect spiritual serenity. I suppose they are saints of sorts … the kind of people in whose presence we intuit the nearness of God because they bring their best friend everywhere with them. God does not accompany them as a bodyguard or go in front of them like a tank clearing a path. He accompanies them like a soprano's pure voice accompanies a song, like a dewdrop on a rose.

One such was Gordon Wilson. He was a man so practised in the discipline of love that when his beautiful daughter Marie died, hard and cruelly, at the slaughter that was the Enniskillen bombing, her hand in his as she slipped away, the words of love and forgiveness sprang as naturally to his lips as a child's eyes are drawn to its mother. His words shamed us, caught us off guard. They seemed so different from what we expected and what we were used to. They brought stillness with them. They carried a sense of the transcendent into a place so ugly we could hardly bear to watch. But he had his detractors, and unbelievably his bags of hate mail. How dare you forgive? they shouted. What

10 Jonathan Sacks (2002), *The Dignity of Difference*, London: Continuum, pp. 188–9, quoting *The Times*, 25 and 26 March.

kind of a father are you who can forgive your daughter's killers? It was as if they had never heard the command to love and forgive anywhere before. It was as if they were being spoken for the first time in the history of humanity and Christ had never uttered the words, 'Father, forgive them for they know not what they do.' As one churchgoing critic said to me on the subject of Gordon Wilson, 'Sure the poor man must have been in shock.' As if to love and offer forgiveness is a sign of mental weakness instead of spiritual strength.[11]

Such stories as these very properly emphasize the importance of individual behaviour in forgiving and seeking the full realization of reconciliation, but there have also been in recent times powerful witnesses to the necessity of forgiveness and reconciliation in public. Martin Luther King, Mahatma Gandhi, Nelson Mandela and Desmond Tutu spring instantly to mind. For reconciliation to be a reality at any level there needs to be the kind of grace, humility, courage, forgiveness and hope that these leaders – and multitudes of ordinary men and women as well – have demonstrated.

In church one Sunday, after the story of the passion of Jesus had been read, my neighbour, a man I had never met, and whose name I did not know, turned to me and said, 'Every time I hear that story, I feel that nothing has changed in this world.'

He was wrong. Something absolutely crucial has been changed. The world is still full of evil and cruelty and violence. But we can now escape from the deadly spirals of vengeance and retaliation, if we take the forgiveness of God seriously. The quality, implications and nature of this forgiveness is wonderfully expressed in a prayer found at Ravensbruck Concentraton Camp beside a dead child on the day of liberation:

> O Lord
> remember not only the men and women of good will,
> but all those of ill will.
> But do not remember all the suffering they have inflicted on us.
> Remember the fruits we have bought thanks to this suffering:
> our comradeship,
> our loyalty,
> our humility,
> our courage,
> our generosity,
> the greatness of heart that has grown out of all this.
> And when they come to judgement,
> let all the fruits we have borne
> be their forgiveness.

11 Desmond Tutu (1999), *No Future Without Forgiveness*, London: Rider, pp.122–3, quoting from Mary McAleese, *Unreconciled Being*.

Postscript: Tsunami Now?

On 26 December 2004, the cataclysmic tsunami devastated the Indian Ocean, tearing apart communities, killing hundreds of thousands of men, women and children – exactly how many will never be known. In minutes dwelling houses, beachside hotels and the huts of poor fishermen and their families were destroyed. It came without warning, and swept aside everything in its way. Comparisons were made with Hiroshima and Nagasaki, but the scale of the devastation was now greater, and responsibility was so much harder to attribute.

It is not surprising that commentators were quick to label the tsunami and its aftermath 'apocalyptic', for indeed natural catastrophes, earthquakes and famines in particular, feature widely in apocalyptic literature, not only as times of great and unprecedented suffering, but also as signs of the end, the 'birth pangs' of a new age. Apocalyptic thus does not only describe natural calamities, but it attempts to give them some fragmentary interpretation, not so much as direct acts of God but rather as the birth pangs of a new order of things, for which disciples may hope even in the face of seeming total disaster. But do not such interpretations seem glib and unconvincing in face of a natural disaster of this magnitude?

How Can One Speak of God after 26 December 2004?

The Archbishop of Canterbury's initial response expressed the mood of many, when he said, 'Every single random accidental death is something that should upset a faith bound up with comfort and ready answers. Faced with the paralysing magnitude of a disaster like this, we naturally feel more deeply outraged and also more deeply helpless.'[1] There are indeed no easy answers on offer, but believers, like everyone else, have to struggle to see how faith, if it survives, might relate to the tragedy, and how people of faith might most appropriately respond. There is no escaping this dual challenge, and there is always the possibility that apocalyptic events such as the tsunami might purify and deepen true faith, while destroying quick and glib parodies of faith.

---

1   *The Times*, 3 January 2005.

I was completing the reflections in this book on faith in a time of terror when the tsunami struck. This was a quite different sort of terror from that generated by 9/11 and its dreadful aftermath. Now it was a disaster which was not in any sense under human control; human decisions were not responsible for it, and although humans and societies could, and did, help with relief and reconstruction, the question was unavoidable. Where was God in all this? Out of this huge disaster and evil there may have come some little, but nonetheless significant, good things – acts of generosity and courage, a new sense of global solidarity and shared responsibility, deeds of kindness – but that in a way simply highlights the question, 'Where was God in all this?' For the good things were human responses to the disaster, the awesome evil was 'an act of God'. Or was it? Here was terrible suffering which was not attributable to human sinfulness, disobedience or moral apathy. It is not surprising that people all around the world ask, 'How can one speak of God after the tsunami?' Is it any longer possible to believe in a creator God who makes and guides the world in love?

Since the 1940s, people have asked in agony, 'How can one speak of God after Auschwitz?' 'How could God have allowed all this?' multitudes cried after the revelation of the full horror of the Holocaust. However hard one struggles with the question, no simple, easy or fully convincing answer is possible, but the question must still be struggled with, and not only by those who strive to remain believers in a God of love. Indeed it is the great question of whether goodness exists and in any sense at all holds sway in the world. Primo Levi, who was a prisoner at Auschwitz, saw the liberating Russian soldiers approaching the camp as he was burying a fellow inmate. Even liberation was for him a mixed experience. 'For us,' he wrote, 'even the hour of liberty rang out grave and muffled, and filled our souls with joy and yet also with a painful sense of pudency, and also with anguish … because we felt that nothing could ever happen good and pure enough to rub out our past, and that the scars of the outrage would remain within us for ever …'[2] And if unspeakable evil which is the direct result of human sin, hideous acts for which human beings are responsible, can shake faith as deeply as this, what of 'acts of God'?

'How can we speak of God after Auschwitz?' is a searing question which has echoed again and again in the modern world. How can we speak of God after the Gulag in which millions died? How can we speak of God after Hiroshima and Nagasaki? How can we speak of God after the Rwanda genocide, when some 800 000 Tutsis died, in which some priests and religious leaders took an active part in the slaughter, while the UN and neighbouring nations did nothing? How can we speak of God after Srebrenica, in which hundreds of innocents were massacred while the world

---

2   Cited by Stephen Phelan in the *Sunday Herald*, 9 January 2005.

watched, as if impotent and helpless? These are hard questions, even for believers who are aware of the power of sin. But how much harder it is to affirm one's faith in a loving and creative God in the face of an unprecedentedly vast natural disaster such as the tsunami.

Many people raged against God in reaction to the tsunami. Or they argued. Or they wept. Or they protested. And in this they resembled Job in the Hebrew Scriptures. God has listened to Job, as he hurls angry accusations at the God who has, he believes, been responsible for the unmerited sufferings that have befallen him. Then God tells Job not to talk but to listen. 'Now I will question you, and you will listen: Where were you when I laid the foundation of the earth? Tell me if you have understanding. Who determined its measurements – surely you know!'[3] We are creatures, and God is God. Our understanding is limited and confused, but we must, like Job and many another, cry out to God in all our fear and anger, and listen to what he has to say.

The tsunami raises huge problems for Christians, and indeed for religious believers of all sorts who do not regard their faith as a very private thing, securely locked into their subjectivity and without salience in the created world. Another common religious response, to the effect that all things come from God, and we should simply be resigned to God's inscrutable will whatever may be, is no more acceptable to those who believe in a God of love. If we label the tsunami an 'act of God', what kind of savage God can we be thinking of? For Christians who believe that God is the loving and almighty creator, not only the tsunami but every death of a child, every death from cancer is a problem with no glib and easy answer possible. Believers as well as unbelievers cry out, 'Why?' and they find no easy answer. How we can speak of God after 26 December 2004 is thus a harder question than how we can speak of God after 9/11. There is no tidy and complete answer possible, but perhaps some hints and fragments from the religious tradition may help a little.

God Almighty

The classical Christian creeds all confess faith in the 'almightiness' of God, and most believers presumably understand this to mean an abstract omnipotence: God can do anything he wishes, and everything that happens comes from God.[4] I well remember a learned German theologian discoursing authoritatively some years ago at an ecumenical conference on

---

3   Job 38.2,4.
4   For a more extended discussion, see chapter 6 of my *Truthful Action: Explorations in Practical Theology*, Edinburgh: T.&T. Clark, 2000.

the omnipotence, or almightiness of God. A metropolitan from Ethiopia, dressed in a long black cassock and with half-a-dozen elaborate pectoral crosses around his neck, and a kind of black pancake on his head, stood up, and interrupted the German theologian in full flow, saying in a loud voice, '*Pantokrator* does not mean *omnipotens*'. Then he sat down. The German theologian blustered, '*Pantokrator*, of course, is Greek; *omnipotens* is Latin', and then he launched once again into his learned disquisition. The Ethiopian Metropolitan rose to his feet once more, this time visibly angry. Clasping his arms in front of him as if to cradle a baby, and rocking gently from side to side, he declared '*Pantokrator*, as all the Greek Fathers affirm, means that God holds the whole world lovingly in his arms and protects it as a mother her child. God is not an arbitrary despot. But God has the power he needs to care for the world.' When the Metropolitan sat down there was silence for a time, even from the German theologian.

And now in the Faith and Order text, *Confessing the One Faith*, these words are to be found:

> Authority and dominion belong to the Fatherhood of God. The Father God is the one who rules and wields authority over all creation, 'the Almighty'. The term used in the Creed is Pantokrator, literally, 'the one who holds and governs all things'. It does not mean 'one who can do anything he wants' in an unqualified way, but rather 'one in whose hands all things are. It is less a description of absolute omnipotence than of universal providence. To call the Father Pantokrator is to affirm that the whole universe is in his grasp, that he does not, and will not, let it go. At the same time it brings with it [at least in principle] the dethroning of all other claimants to universal sovereignty, to government and mastery over the world and its history and destiny ... Faith in God's omnipotence gives confidence that 'the powers of the present age' – whether political, economic, scientific, industrial, military, ideological or indeed religious – do not control and will not have the last word concerning the destiny of the world and humankind. The Lordship of the Almighty relativises and judges them all; it confronts all other claims to sovereignty, it is a challenge to every form of enslaving bondage ... To confess the Lordship of the Almighty is to celebrate the liberating strength of the Creator and to proclaim hope for each individual and for the whole universe ... The confession of God's omnipotence does not mean that he is to be conceived as a coercive and all-powerful tyrant. Rather, God's power is the power of creative love and of loving concern for creatures.[5]

Such a linking of power and care through rooting it in the very nature of God is surely suggestive and helpful. Karl Barth reminded his listeners in Bonn just after the end of the Second World War that Adolph Hitler had

---

5 *Confessing the One Faith*, Faith and Order Paper 153, Geneva: World Council of Churches, 1991, p.33.

characteristically and constantly referred to God as 'the Almighty'. But that, said Barth, is a fundamental distortion. If God is power in itself, then he must be bad. We cannot and must not understand God in the light of an otherwise determined understanding of power; we must rather understand power in the light of what we know of God.[6]

All this theologizing may be important, but it still does not answer to the despair and uncertainty evoked by a disaster such as the tsunami. If God indeed has the will and the power to shelter his people in his arms, as the Ethiopian metropolitan suggested, why did he not do it on this occasion? Are God's power and love indeed such as Christian believers suggest? What of God's power when natural forces seem to be able to snatch millions from his grasp?

Father and Creator

God in Jesus limits his power and shares in the sufferings of the world. And Jesus taught his followers to approach God as Father, and indeed to use in prayer the intimate, informal Aramaic term, *Abba*, or 'Daddy', rather than the more formal Greek *Pater*. He declared, 'It is not the will of your Father in heaven that one of these little ones should be lost.'[7] The God who is our *Abba* is the creator, and we rejoice in the wonder, beauty and power of the universe God has created in all its intrinsic marvellousness, and its immensity. We look at the stars and we wonder. God, we read in the creation stories in Genesis, created the world and saw that it was very good. And its goodness reflects the goodness of God:

> The heavens are telling the glory of God;
> and the firmament proclaims his handiwork.
> Day to day pours forth speech,
> and night to night declares knowledge.
> There is no speech, nor are there words;
> their voice is not heard;
> yet their voice goes out through all the earth;
> and their words to the end of the world.
> In the heavens he has set a tent for the sun,
> which comes out like a bridegroom from his wedding canopy,
> and like a strong man runs its course with joy.
> Its rising is from the end of the heavens,
> and its circuit to the end of them; and nothing is hidden from its heat.[8]

6   Karl Barth (1949), *Dogmatics in Outline*, London: SCM Press, pp.47–9.
7   Matthew 18.14.
8   Psalm 19.1–6.

And the psalmist proclaims:

> O Lord, our Sovereign,
> how majestic is your name in all the earth!
> When I look at your heavens, the work of your fingers,
> the moon and stars that you have established,
> what are human beings that you are mindful of them,
> mortals that you care for them?
>
> Yet you have made them a little lower than God,
> and crowned them with glory and honour.
> You have given them dominion over the works of your hands,
> you have put all things under their feet,
> all sheep and oxen,
> and also the beasts of the field,
> the birds of the air, and the fish of the sea,
> whatever passes along the paths of the seas.
> O Lord, our Sovereign,
> How majestic is your name in all the earth![9]

Yet is this Creator God indeed mindful of mortals? Does God really care for them, for us? And has God given effective dominion and responsibility for the creation to human beings? The tsunami was indeed independent of human control or human causation. We are not responsible for it, although we have responsibilities in regard to the way we respond to the distress and suffering and devastation that it caused.

The Faultline in Creation

The Bible witnesses to the fallenness, the brokenness of the creation that was initially declared by God to be 'very good'. In the mythological language of Genesis, chapter 3, we are no longer in Eden, but in a fractured and often callous world that is now not fully under the loving control of the God who made it all and in the beginning saw that it was very good. There is a fatal flaw, so that we often experience the creation, not so much as glorious, but as 'nature red in tooth and claw', as hostile and threatening, as in the tsunami. As the great Scottish churchman, George MacLeod wrote in one of his remarkable prayers, 'The Whole Earth Shall Cry Glory':

> But creation is not enough.
> Always in the beauty, the foreshadowing of decay.
> The lambs frolicking careless: so soon to be led off to slaughter.

---

9 Psalm 8.1, 3–8.

Nature red and scarred as well as lush and green.
In the garden also:
always the thorn.
Creation is not enough.[10]

The creation, for all its glory, is still fallen, as we see most clearly in awesome and awful events such as the tsunami. It needs redemption and transformation, just as we do. In Paul's dramatic words, the whole creation, which has been subject to futility and decay, and is 'groaning in labour pains', eagerly longs for the time when the sufferings of today, awful as they are, are submerged in the glory that is to come, and for which we hope.[11]

The great disaster of the cross was understood by the Church from the beginning to be the pivotal moment in the redemption of humankind – and the creation, too, is to be redeemed. As the sixth-century hymn writer, Venantius Fortunatus, put it:

> Sing, my tongue, how glorious battle
> Glorious victory became;
> And above the cross, his trophy,
> Tell the triumph and the fame:
> Tell how he, the earth's Redeemer,
> By his death for man o'ercame.
>
> His the nails, the spear, the spitting,
> Reed and vinegar and gall;
> From his patient body pierced
> Blood and water streaming fall;
> *Earth and seas and stars and mankind*
> *By that stream are cleansed all.*[12]

Responding to Disaster

The initial reaction to news of the tsunami was extraordinary. Out of all the grief, and pain and suffering, out of all the uncertainty and fear, there came, at least initially, unparalleled generosity from all around the world. The liberality of ordinary citizens shamed governments into generosity. Relief supplies, and promises of help in reconstruction, flowed from the prosperous countries to the affected areas round the Indian Ocean. It was as if a new worldwide human solidarity had emerged from the cataclysm. ✗

---

10   George F. MacLeod (1985), *The Whole Earth Shall Cry Glory*, Iona: Wild Goose Publications, p.8.
11   Romans 8.16–27.
12   *The Church Hymnary*, 3rd edn, no. 256; my italics.

✗ Not so good after the Kashmir earthquake, Oct. 2005!

There are, of course, worries about possible corruption, about whether promises of assistance will actually be realized, about the difficulty of getting supplies to where they are most needed in time. An 'act of God' that is devastating and that aroused terror around the world also stimulated immense generosity. But there is a serious problem hidden here: some problems in today's world are far more devastating and large-scale than the tsunami, but because they are scattered and sometimes invisible, they stimulate neither the anger nor the generosity that the tsunami aroused. And these are problems for which human beings, states and companies are responsible, and which could be resolved by determined efforts. Think of the vast numbers affected by the HIV/AIDS pandemic, especially in Africa, and think also of the awful statistic verified by the UN and leading development NGOs, that every single day some 30 000 children die of starvation and malnutrition-related diseases.

Would that these problems, created by human beings and human organizations, could be tackled with the same determination – and anger that children should suffer so. For Jesus said, 'It is not the will of your Father in heaven that one of these little ones should be lost.'[13]

We cannot explain adequately the disaster of the tsunami. We cannot explain adequately the disaster, the wondrous disaster of the crucified God. We rest our slender faith on that earthly disaster that was a heavenly triumph. But the disaster of 30 000 children dying from poverty each day, and multitudes suffering from the effects of HIV/AIDS, are things that we can in fact affect for good, and so make a difference.

Perhaps I can best sum up this reflection with a prayer by my friend, John Bell, which he used during a special BBC *Songs of Praise* Vigil for the tsunami, for these times of terror:

> We have learned a new word – tsunami –
> which you already knew, Lord,
> for you created this world
> in all its beauty and terror.
> Hallowed be your name.
>
> If in these past days we have not hallowed you,
> if we have cursed heaven and asked why,
> and expressed horror and confusion in equal measure,
> do not hold it against us.
> Take it as the worship of our sorrow,
> for you meant us to care and not to be neutral.

---

13   Matthew 18.14.

What shall we pray for what we cannot understand?
Words are too thin to cradle this complexity.
So, if we are silent,
it is not to show indifference,
but to show solidarity with those
who are homeless, hopeless, speechless.

For those who suffer in body, soul and mind,
    let there be deep healing;
for those who grieve, especially in the absence of a body to bury,
    let there be deep consolation;
for those who have died, may there be a safe landing
    on another shore.

And let there be angels, in divine and human form,
to help hold together the broken bits of lives,
to listen to stories which begin with the ending
    and go no further,
to light a candle rather than curse the darkness.

And may we all resolve
to revere this fragile earth rather than abuse it,
to enable developing nations rather than indebt them,
and to claim your presence
rather than fear your absence
at the heart of every storm.

Bibliography

Ackerman, Bruce A. (1980), *Social Justice in the Liberal State*, New Haven: Yale University Press.

Ackermann, Denise (1992), 'The Alchemy of Hope' in Dennis Brutus (ed.), *A Book of Hope*, Claremont, RSA: David Philip.

Aquinas, St Thomas (1969), *Summa Theologiae*, vol. 23: *Virtue*, 1a2ae. 55–67, London: Blackfriars.

———— (1973), *"The Summa Theologica" of St Thomas Aquinas*, vol. 13 (Second Part of the Second Part, QQ. CXLI–CLXX), London: Burns Oates and Washbourne.

Arendt, Hannah (1958), *The Human Condition*, Chicago: University of Chicago Press.

Armstrong, Karen (2000), *The Battle for God: Fundamentalism in Judaism, Christianity and Islam*, London: HarperCollins.

Ateek, Naim (2002), 'Suicide Bombers: A Palestinian Christian Perspective', in *Voices from the Third World*, **XXV** (1 & 2), pp.121–50.

———— (2004), *Suicide Bombers: What is theologically and morally wrong with suicide bombings?*, Jerusalem: Sabeel Ecumenical Liberation Theology Centre.

Audi, Robert (2000), *Religious Commitment and Secular Reason*, Cambridge: Cambridge University Press.

———— and Nicholas Wolterstorff (1997), *Religion in the Public Square: The Place of Religious Convictions in Political Debate*, Lanham: Rowman and Littlefield Publishers.

Barth, Karl (1949), *Dogmatics in Outline*, London: SCM Press.

Bauckham, R. and T. Hart (eds) (1997), *Hope Against Hope*, London: Darton, Longman and Todd.

Bauckham, Richard (1993a), *The Climax of Prophecy: Studies in the Book of Revelation*, Edinburgh: T.&T. Clark.

———— (1993b), *The Theology of the Book of Revelation*, Cambridge: Cambridge University Press.

———— (2001), 'Revelation', in John Barton and John Muddiman (eds), *The Oxford Bible Commentary*, Oxford: Oxford University Press, pp.1287–8.

———— (2002), *God and the Crisis of Freedom*, Louisville: Westminster John Knox Press.

———— (2004), 'Freedom in the Crisis of Modernity', in Andrew Morton and William Storrar (eds), *Public Theology for the 21st Century*, London: Continuum.

Bauman, Zygmunt (1991), *Modernity and the Holocaust*, Ithaca: Cornell University Press.

——— (1995), *Life in Fragments: Essays in Postmodern Morality*, Oxford: Blackwell.

Belloc, Hilaire (1962), *Europe and the Faith*, London: Burns and Oates.

Berger, Peter (ed.) (1999), *The Desecularization of the World: Resurgent Religion and World Politics*, Grand Rapids: Eerdmans.

Biggar, Nigel (1987), 'Any News of What's Good for Society?', *Latimer Comment*, 24, Oxford.

——— (ed.) (2001), *Burying the Past: Making Peace and Doing Justice after Civil Conflict*, Washington: Georgetown University Press.

——— (2004), 'Anglican Theology of War and Peace', *Crucible*, Oct.–Dec.

Bishop, Peter D. (1981), *A Technique for Loving: Non-violence in Indian and Christian Traditions*, London: SCM.

Boesak, Alan (1987), *Comfort and Protest: the Apocalypse from a South African Perspective*, Philadelphia: Westminster.

Boraine, Alex (2000), *A Country Unmasked*, Oxford: Oxford University Press.

Borradori, Giovanna (2003), *Philosophy in a Time of Terror: Dialogues with Jürgen Habermas and Jacques Derrida*, Chicago: University of Chicago Press.

Brook, Wes Howard and Anthony Gwyther (1999), *Unveiling Empire: Reading Revelation Then and Now*, Maryknoll: Orbis.

Brown, Charles (1992), *Niebuhr and His Age*, Philadelphia: Trinity Press.

Browning, Robert L. and Roy A. Reed (eds) (2004), *Forgiveness, Reconciliation and Moral Courage*, Grand Rapids: Eerdmans.

Bruce, Steve (2000a), *Fundamentalism*, Cambridge: Polity Press.

——— (2000b), 'Zealot Politics and Democracy: The Case of the New Christian Right', *Political Studies*, **48**, 263–82.

Buckley, James and L. Gregory Jones (eds) (2001), *Theology and Eschatology: At the Turn of the Millennium*, Oxford: Blackwell.

Busch, E. (1976), *Karl Barth: His Life from Letters and Autobiographical Texts*, London: SCM Press.

Cameron, Averil (1999), 'On the Grace of Humility', *Theology*, March/April.

Casanova, José (1995), *Public Religions in the Modern World*, Chicago: University of Chicago Press.

Chase, Kenneth R. and Alan Jacobs (eds) (2003), *Must Christianity be Violent? Reflections on History, Practice and Theology*, Grand Rapids: Brazos.

Chaucer, Geoffrey (1951), *The Canterbury Tales*, trans. by Neville Coghill, Harmondsworth: Penguin.

Chernus, Ira (2004), 'George W. Bush's War on Terrorism and Sin', *Political Theology*, **5** (4), pp.411–30.

Chomsky, N. (2003), *Middle East Illusions*, Lanham: Bowman and Littlefield.

Cohen, Mark R. and Peter Schäfer (eds) (1998), *Towards the Millenium: Messianic Expectations from the Bible to Waco*, Leiden: Brill.

Cohn, Norman (1970), *The Pursuit of the Millennium*, London: Paladin.

────── (1993), *Cosmos, Chaos and the World to Come: The Ancient Roots of Apocalyptic Faith*, New Haven: Yale University Press.

Collins, Adela Yarbro (1984), *Crisis and Catharsis: The Power of the Apocalypse*, Philadelphia: Westminster.

Collins, John J. (1998), *The Apocalyptic Imagination: An Introduction to Jewish Apocalyptic Literature*, 2nd edn, Grand Rapids: Eerdmans.

Davie, Grace (2002), *Europe: The Exceptional Case*, London: Darton, Longman and Todd.

Derrida, Jacques (2001), 'On Forgiveness', in *Cosmopolitanism and Forgiveness*, London: Routledge.

Derrida, Jacques (2001), *Cosmopolitanism and Forgiveness*, London: Routledge.

Ecumenical Review (2003), 'Religion and Violence: An Inter-religious Exploration', **55** (2).

Eliot, T.S. (1968), *Murder in the Cathedral*, London: Faber and Faber.

Ellis, Marc H. (1997), *Unholy Alliance: Religion and Atrocity in Our Time*, Minneapolis: Fortress Press.

Ellul, Jacques (1977), *Apocalypse: The Book of Revelation*, New York: Seabury.

Elshtain, Jean Bethke (1988), 'Citizenship and Armed Virtue: Some Questions on the Commitment to Public Life', in Charles H. Reynolds and Ralph Norman (eds), *Community in America: The Challenge of Habits of the Heart*, Berkeley: University of California Press.

────── (2003), *Just War Against Terror: The Burden of American Power in a Violent World*, New York: Basic Books.

Esposito, John L. (2002), *Unholy War: Terror in the Name of Islam*, Oxford: Oxford University Press.

Etzioni, Amitai (2004), *From Empire to Community: A New Approach to International Relations*, New York: Macmillan Palgrave.

Falconer, Alan D. and Joseph Liechty (eds) (1998), *Reconciling Memories*, Dublin: Columba.

Forester, John (1989), *Planning in the Face of Power*, Berkeley: University of California Press.

Forrester, Duncan B. (1985), *Christianity and the Future of Welfare*, London: Epworth.

────── (1989), *Beliefs, Values and Policies*, Oxford: Clarendon Press.

────── (1997), *Christian Justice and Public Policy*, Cambridge: Cambridge University Press.

────── (2000), *Truthful Action: Explorations in Practical Theology*, Edinburgh: T.&T. Clark.

────── (2001), *On Human Worth. A Christian Vindication of Equality*, London: SCM Press.

Freeden, Michael (2000), 'Practising Ideology and Ideological Practices', *Political Studies*, **48**, 302–22.

Friedrich, Carl J. (ed.) (1949), *The Philosophy of Kant: Immanuel Kant's Moral and Political Writings*, New York: Random House.

Frykenberg, Robert E. (ed.) (2003), *Christians and Missonaries in India*, Grand Rapids: Eerdmans.

Fukuyama, Francis (1989), 'The End of History', *The National Interest*, **16** (Summer).

——— (1993), *The End of History and the Last Man*, New York: Avon Books.

——— (2002), 'Their Target: The Modern World', *Newsweek* (February).

Gandhi, M.K. (1961), *Non-violent Resistance*, New York: Schocken.

Garrison, J. (1980), *From Hiroshima to Harrisburg*, London: SCM.

Gascoigne, Robert (2001), *The Public Forum and Christian Ethics*, Cambridge: Cambridge University Press.

Gilbert, Paul (2003), *New Terror, New Wars*, Edinburgh: Edinburgh University Press.

Gill, David (ed.) (1983), *Gathered for Life: Official Report, VI Assembly of the World Council of Churches*, Geneva: WCC.

Girard, René (1977), *Violence and the Sacred*, Baltimore: Johns Hopkins University Press.

Gittings, John (1991), *Beyond the Gulf War: The Middle East and the New World Order*, London: CIIR.

Glendon, Mary Anne and David Blankenhorn (eds) (1995), *Seedbeds of Virtue: Sources of Competence, Character and Citizenship in American Society*, Lanham: Madison Books.

Gopin, Marx (2000), *Between Eden and Armageddon: The Future of World Religions, Violence and Peacemaking*, Oxford: Oxford University Press.

Gorringe, Timothy (1996), *God's Just Vengeance: Crime, Violence and the Rhetoric of Salvation*, Cambridge: Cambridge University Press.

Gray, John (2002), 'Why terrorism is unbeatable', *The New Statesman*, 25 February.

——— (2003), *Al Qaeda and What It Means to be Modern*, London: Faber and Faber.

Griffith, Lee (2002), *The War on Terrorism and the Terror of God*, Grand Rapids: Eerdmans, 220–21.

Gruchy, John W. de (2002), *Reconciliation: Restoring Justice*, London: SCM Press.

Guthrie, W.K.C. (1971), *Socrates*, Cambridge: Cambridge University Press, pp.130–39.

Habermas, Jürgen (2003), *The Future of Human Nature*, Cambridge: Polity.

Hampson, Daphne (1986), 'Reinhold Niebuhr on Sin: A Critique', in Richard Harries (ed.), *Reinhold Niebuhr and the Issues of Our Time*, London: Mowbray, p.47.

Harrison, Carol (2000), *Augustine: Christian Truth and Fractured Humanity*, Oxford: Oxford University Press.

Harvie, A.E. (2001), *By What Authority?*, London: SCM.

Hastings, Adrian (1986), *A History of English Christianity 1920–1985*, London: Jonathan Cape.

Hauerwas, Stanley and Charles Pinches (1997), *Christians Among the Virtues: Theological Conversations with Ancient and Modern Ethics*, Notre Dame: University of Notre Dame Press.

Havel, Vaclav (1987), *Living in Truth*, London: Faber.

Hinchliffe, Peter (1982), *Holiness in Politics*, London: Darton, Longman and Todd.

Holmes, Arthur F. (1975), *War and Christian Ethics*, Grand Rapids: Baker Book House.

Honderich, Ted (2002), *After the Terror*, Edinburgh: Edinburgh University Press.

Horsley, Richard A. (1987), *Jesus and the Spiral of Violence: Popular Jewish Resistance in Roman Palestine*, San Francisco: Harper and Row.

—————— (ed.) (1997), *Paul and Empire: Religion and Power in Roman Imperial Society*, Harrisburg: Trinity Press.

—————— (2003a), *Jesus and Empire: the Kingdom of God and the New World Disorder*, Minneapolis: Fortress.

—————— (2003b), *Religion and Empire: People, Power and the Life of the Spirit*, Minneapolis: Fortress.

Howard, Michael (2001), 'Mistake to Declare this a War', *Royal United Services Institute Journal*, Dec. 2001.

Hull, John (2002), *Religion and Terror in the Modern World: The Educational Responsibility of the Church*, Edinburgh: Church of Scotland Education Committee.

Huntington, Samuel P. (1996), *The Clash of Civilizations and the Remaking of World Order*, New York: Touchstone.

—————— (2002), 'The Age of Muslim Wars', *Newsweek*, Dec. 2001–Feb. 2002.

Hutton, Will (2003), *The World We're In*, London: Abacus.

Ignatieff, Michael (2003), 'The Lesser Evil: Political Ethics in an Age of Terror', Gifford Lectures in the University of Edinburgh, lecture 5 (typescript).

Jehle, Frank (2002), *Ever Against the Stream: The Politics of Karl Barth, 1906–1968*, Grand Rapids: Eerdmans.

John Paul II (1991), *Centesimus Annus* (Encyclical Letter), London: CTS.

Johnson, J.T. (1981), *Just War Tradition and the Restraint of War*, Princeton: Princeton University Press.

Johnston, Douglas and Cynthia Sampson (eds) (1994), *Religion – The Missing Dimension of Statecraft*, Oxford: OUP.

Juergensmeyer, Mark (2001), *Terror in the Mind of God: The Global Rise of Religious Violence*, Berkeley: University of California Press.

Junck, Robert (1960), *Brighter Than a Thousand Suns*, Harmondsworth: Penguin.

Kagan, Robert (2003), *Paradise and Power: America and Europe in the New World Order*, London: Atlantic.

Kaplan, Robert D. (2003), *Warrior Politics: Why Leadership Demands a Pagan Ethos*, New York: Vintage Books.

Kässmann Margot (1998), *Overcoming Violence: The Challenge to the Churches in All Places*, Geneva: WCC.

Keane, John (1998), 'The Limits of Secularism: Does the Marginalizing of Religion Impose a New Intolerance?', *Times Literary Supplement*, 9 Jan., pp.12–13.

——— (2004), *Violence and Democracy*, Cambridge: Cambridge University Press.

Keenan, Brian (1992), *An Evil Cradling*, London: Hutchison.

Kepel, Gilles (1994), *Revenge of God: The Resurgence of Islam, Christianity and Judaism in the Modern World*, University Park, PA: Pennsylvania State University Press.

——— (2002), *Jihad: The Trail of Political Islam*, Cambridge, MA: Harvard University Press.

Kovacs, Judith and Christopher Rowland (2004), *Revelation*, Oxford: Blackwell.

Küng, Hans (1991), *Global Responsibility: In Search of a New World Ethic*, London: SCM Press.

——— (1997), *A Global Ethic for Global Politics and Economics*, London: SCM Press.

——— and Helmut Schmidt (1998), *A Global Ethic and Global Responsibilities: Two Declarations*, London: SCM Press.

Leonard, Stephen T. (1990), *Critical Theory in Political Practice*, Princeton: Princeton University Press.

Lewis, Bernard (2003a), *The Crisis of Islam: Holy War and Unholy Terror*, London: Orion.

——— (2003b), *What Went Wrong? Western Impact and Middle Eastern Response*, London: Phoenix.

Lincoln, Bruce (2003), *Holy Terrors: Thinking about Religion after September 11*, Chicago: University of Chicago Press.

Luther, Martin (1931), 'Whether Soldiers, too, can be Saved', in *Works of Martin Luther*, vol. 5, Philadelphia: A.J. Holman Company, pp.34–74.

Lyotard, J.-F. (1997), *Postmodern Fables*, Minneapolis: University of Minnesota Press.

MacIntyre, Alastair (1981), *After Virtue: A Study in Moral Theory*, London: Duckworth, p.171.

MacLeod, George F. (1985), *The Whole Earth Shall Cry Glory*, Iona: Wild Goose Publications.

Magnusson, Magnus and Hermann Palsson (trans.) (1969), *Laxdaela Saga*, Harmondsworth: Penguin.

McCarthy, John (2001), 'Introduction' to Matthew Sturgis (ed.), *It Ain't Necessarily So*, London: Headline.

Meilaender, Gilbert C. (1984), *The Theory and Practice of Virtue*, Notre Dame: University of Notre Dame Press.

Melden, A.I. (ed.) (1958), *Essays in Moral Philosophy*, Seattle: University of Washington Press.

Miller, Richard B. (2002), 'Aquinas and the Presumption against Killing and War', *The Journal of Religion*, pp.173–204.

Minow, Martha (1998), *Between Vengeance and Forgiveness*, Boston: Beacon Press.

———— (ed.) (2002), *Breaking the Cycles of Hatred: Memory, Law and Repair*, Princeton: Princeton University Press.

Moore, Edward (1878), *An Introduction to Aristotle's Ethics*, 2nd edn, Oxford: Rivingtons.

Morton, A. (ed.) (1998), *A Turning Point in Ireland and Scotland? The Challenge to the Churches and to Theology Today*, Edinburgh, CTPI.

Morton, Andrew and William Storrar (eds) (2004), *Public Theology for the 21st Century*, London: Continuum.

Murphy, Nancey, Brad J. Kallenberg and Mark Theissen Nation (eds) (1997), *Virtues and Practices in the Christian Tradition: Christian Ethics After MacIntyre*, Notre Dame: University of Notre Dame Press.

Newbigin, Lesslie (1982), *The Light Has Come*, Grand Rapids: Eerdmans.

Niebuhr, Reinhold (1941, 1943), *The Nature and Destiny of Man*, London: Nisbet.

———— (1945), *The Children of Light and the Children of Darkness*, London: Nisbet.

———— (1947), 'America's Precarious Eminence', *The Virginia Quarterly Review* (Autumn).

Northcott, M.S. (2004a), *An Angel Directs the Storm: Apocalyptic Religion and American Empire*, London: I.B. Tauris.

———— (2004b), 'Bringing on the Apocalypse', *Third Way*, Nov., pp.22–4.

O'Donovan, Oliver (2000), review of Hans Küng and Helmut Schmidt, *A Global Ethic and Global Responsibilities: Two Declarations*, in *Studies in Christian Ethics*, **13** (1), pp.122–8.

———— (2003), *The Just War Revisited*, Cambridge: Cambridge University Press.

O'Neill, Brendan (2004), 'Terrorists: People who are just like us', *New Statesman*, 26 July.

Palsson, Herman and Paul Edwards (trans.) (1981), *Orkneyinga Saga*, Harmondsworth: Penguin.

Partner, Peter (1997), *God of Battles: Holy Wars of Christianity and Islam*, London: HarperCollins.

Partridge, Christopher H. (2001), *Fundamentalisms*, Carlisle: Paternoster Press.

Pastoral Letters, US Catholic Bishops (1983), *The Challenge of Peace: God's Promise and Our Response*, London: CTS/SPCK.

Pentland, Ray (2002), 'Just War – Just Sanctions', *Political Theology*, **2** (3).

Pieper, Josef (1955), *Fortitude and Temperance*, London: Faber and Faber.

Pinches, Charles (2000), 'Virtue', in Adrian Hastings (ed.), *The Oxford Companion to Christian Thought*, Oxford: Clarendon.

Plant, Raymond (2001), *Politics, Theology and History*, Cambridge: Cambridge University Press.

Plaskow, Judith (1980), *Sex, Sin and Grace: Women's Experience and the Theologies of Reinhold Niebuhr and Paul Tillich*, Lanham, MD: University Press of America.

Porter, Jean (1990), *The Recovery of Virtue*, Louisville: Westminster/John Knox.

Powers, Gerard F. et al. (eds) (1993), *Peacemaking: Moral and Policy Challenges for a New World*, Washington, DC: United States Catholic Conference.

Ramsey, Paul (1968), *The Just War: Force and Political Responsibility*, Lanham: University Press of America.

Rawls, J. (1972), *A Theory of Justice*, Oxford: Oxford University Press.

——— (1985), 'Justice as Fairness: Political not Metaphysical', *Philosophy and Public Affairs*, **14** (3), 223–51.

——— (1993), *Political Liberalism*, New York: Columbia University Press.

——— (1999), *The Law of Peoples with 'The Idea of Public Reason Revisited'*, Cambridge, MA: Harvard University Press.

Ross, Sir David (1954), *The Nichomathean Ethics of Aristotle*, Oxford: Oxford University Press.

Rowland, Christopher (1982), *The Open Heaven: A Study of Apocalyptic in Judaism and Early Christianity*, London: SPCK.

——— (1988), *Radical Christianity*, Cambridge: Polity.

Rowley, H.H. (1947), *The Relevance of Apocalyptic*, London: Lutterworth.

Ruthven, Malise (2002), *A Fury for God: The Islamist Attack on America*, London: Granta Books.

Sacks, Jonathan (2002), *The Dignity of Difference*, London: Continuum.

Schall, James V. (2000), '*Fides et Ratio*: Approaches to a Roman Catholic Political Philosophy', *The Review of Politics*, **62** (1).

Schlosberg, David (1995), 'Communicative Action in Practice: Intersubjectivity and New Social Movements', *Political Studies*, XLIII.

Shriver, Donald W. (1995), *An Ethic for Enemies: Forgiveness in Politics*, New York: Oxford University Press.

Sick, Gary (1985), *All Fall Down: America's Tragic Encounter with Iran*, New York: Penguin, pp.192–3.

Stassen, Glen H. (ed.) (1992), *Just Peacemaking: Transforming Initiatives for Justice and Peace*, Louisville: Westminster/John Knox.

Stassen, Glen H. (2004), 'Just Peacemaking as Hermeneutical Key: The Need for International Co-operation in Preventing Terrorism', *Journal of the Society of Christian Ethics*, **24** (2), pp.171–91.

Stiltner, Brian (1999), *Religion and the Common Good: Catholic Contributions to Building Community in a Liberal Society*, Lanham, MD: Rowman and Littlefield.

————— (2000), 'Reassessing Religion's Place in a Liberal Democracy', *Religious Studies Review*, **26** (4) (October), 319–25.

Stout, Jeffrey (2004), *Democracy and Tradition*, Princeton: Princeton University Press.

Taylor, Charles (1983), *Social Theory as Practice*, Delhi: Oxford University Press.

Tertullian (1869–70), *Apologeticus* 39; *De Corona* 13, in *The Writings of Tertullian*, Ante-Nicene Christian Library, 3 vols, Edinburgh: T. & T. Clark.

The National Security Strategy of the United States of America (2002), Washington, DC, September.

Theissen, Gerd (1999), *A Theory of Primitive Christianity*, London: SCM Press.

Thompson, Leonard H. (1990), *The Book of Revelation: Apocalypse and Empire*, New York: Oxford University Press.

Townshend, Charles (2002), *Terrorism: A Very Short Introduction*, Oxford: Oxford University Press.

Tutu, Desmond (1999), *No Future Without Forgiveness*, London: Rider.

US Catholic Bishops (1994), *The Harvest of Justice is Sown in Peace*.

Utmson, J.O. (1958), 'Saints and Heroes', in A.I. Melden (ed.), *Essays in Moral Philosophy*, Seattle: University of Washington Press.

Waite, Terry (1993), *Taken on Trust*. London: Hodder and Stoughton.

Walzer, Michael (1980), *Just and Unjust Wars: A Moral Argument with Historical Illustrations*, Harmondsworth: Penguin.

Watson, Duane F. (ed.) (2002), *The Intertexture of Apocalyptic Discourse in the New Testament*, Atlanta: SBL.

Weber, Theodore R. (1989), 'Truth and Political Leadership', *Annual of the Society of Christian Ethics*, pp.5–19.

————— (2000), 'Vengeance Denied, Politics Affirmed: Applying the Criterion of "Just Intention"', in *Societas Ethica Jahresbericht*, pp.170–76.

Wells, Samuel (1999), 'The Disarming Virtue of Stanley Hauerwas', *Scottish Journal of Theology*, **52** (1), pp.82–8.

Wicker, Brian (2002), 'Conflict and Martyrdom after 11th September 2001', 0.8: http://website.lineone.net/~ccadd/cta_paper_2002.htm

Williams, Ann (ed.) (1989), *Prophecy and Millenarianism: Essays in Honour of Marjorie Reeves*, London: Longman.

Williams, Rowan (2002), *Writing in the Dust: Reflections on 11th September and its Aftermath*, London: Hodder and Stoughton.

Wilson, H.S. (2002), 'Terrorism and Religions', *Bangalore Theological Forum*, **XXXIV** (June), pp.58–74.

Wilson, Richard A. (2001), *The Politics of Truth and Reconciliation in South Africa*, Cambridge: Cambridge University Press.

Yoder, John Howard (1984), *The Priestly Kingdom: Social Ethics as Gospel*, Notre Dame, ID: University of Notre Dame Press.

———— (1988), 'To Serve our God and to Rule the World', *The Annual of the Society of Christian Ethics*, pp.3–14.

———— (1994), 'Regarding Nature' (unpublished paper drafted and circulated in connection with a Notre Dame course on the Just War Tradition), Notre Dame Collection of John Yoder's Writings, http://www.nd.edu/~theo/jhy/writings/philsystheo/nature.htm

Index

Title for an article, 'The End of Eschatology'.
– a companion-piece to 'In the End, which God?'